BILLY FROM SCRATCH

 www.trafford.com

North America & international
toll-free: 1 888 232 4444 (USA & Canada)
phone: 250 383 6864 ♦ fax: 250 383 6804 ♦ email: info@trafford.com

Dedicated To:

My Beloved Bob,

My Parents,

And All

Of My Family

With

Love and Best Regards

Good things have happened in my life and bad things have happened to me; however; the following introduction is one of the worst things that has ever transpired in my entire life span. The forest fire was burned into my memory. I can see it today as clearly as I could when I was a small child. This is the story from my memory - a true story.

Prologue

Suddenly in the deep dark of night I am wide awake. My hands are clenched – wet with cold sweat. I smell the stench of hungry flames. I hear the deafening noise of raging fire. I see animals running blindly, showing no fear of man, running for their lives. The earth and sky are bright red. I am completely enveloped in the clutches of fear.

Introduction

This is the true story of the first phase of my life. It was a turbulent time, not only in our lives, but in the history of our country. This is a story of survival during the "Great Depression." It was also the time of tenacious rumblings of war from Europe. It was a very unsettled time in America. It was terrifying, and at times overwhelming, yet it was also an awe-inspiring time. It was a time that drew our family even closer together.

This story is from my memory of that time of testing. It is from voiced opinions that I heard from my parents and their co-workers, and friends. Much of the narrative is often told through remembered conversations, which of course, are not remembered word - for - word; however, they do speak of the thinking of that time. Those serious late night talks mirrored the thinking of the working people. These were talks of substance.

This is the story of the common American working man, and his family and friends, through some of the hardest times ever experienced in our country. The only true names are mine and of my parents. All other names have been changed to protect privacy. If there are any errors, they are the sole responsibility of my young memories.

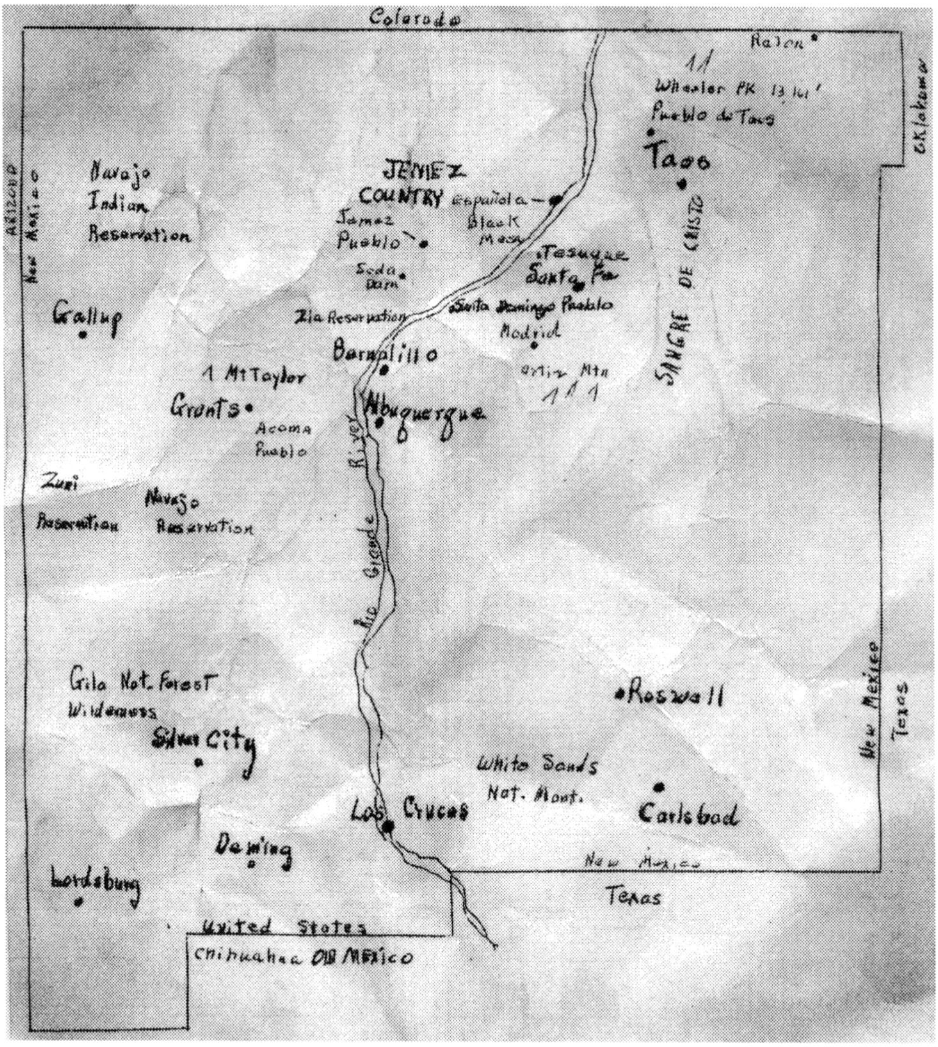

Colorado
Raton
Wheeler PK
Pueblo de Taos
Taos
Oklahoma
Arizona
New Mexico
Navajo
Indian
Reservation
JEMEZ
COUNTRY
Española
Jemez
Pueblo
Black
Mesa
Soda
Dam
Tesuque
Santa Fe
Santo Domingo Pueblo
Madrid
Zia Reservation
SANGRE DE CRISTO
Gallup
Bernalillo
Mt Taylor
Ortiz Mtn
Grants
Albuquerque
Acoma
Pueblo
Zuni
Reservation
Navajo
Reservation
Rio Grande River
Gila Nat. Forest
Wilderness
Roswell
Silver City
White Sands
Nat. Mont.
Las Cruces
Carlsbad
Deming
Lordsburg
New Mexico
Texas
United States
Chihuahua Old Mexico

Chapter 1

My Early Life in the Jemez Mountains

My name is Billy. I was named after my Dad, although that was not his real name.

Dad was fourteen years old at the end of World War I. It was the time of the great flu epidemic, and his sprightly, red-headed mother died in that pandemic. She was forty-three years old. Dad and his sister were the only ones left at home, since both of his older brothers were in Germany in the army. They had both fought through the entire war, and the younger one was seriously injured with mustard gas.

Dad was crushed when his mother died, and he was not fond of his grandmother, who was to be the one looking after him. She only looked after him for one year. Then Dad decided to join the army, and become a man as his older brother's had done when the war had started. He went to the recruiting center.

The Captain in charge looked at my Dad and said, "How old are you, Son?"

At that time, few people had any kind of identification, so Dad boldly answered, "I am almost twenty-one and a half, Sir, and I have no family."

The Captain asked, "Are you sure you want to join the army? You look pretty young to me. You know the war is over, but it is still pretty rough out there. Are you sure of this?"

"Yes Sir, I am sure."

Sit down, Son. We have papers to fill out. Now I can see your eyes are blue. Your hair is light brown, actually almost blond, and curly too."

Dad blushed but he didn't move an inch.

The Captain continued, "I guess I would call your complexion ruddy, let's check your height. That is five feet and ten inches. And the last thing here, what is your occupations?"

"I am an electrician, Sir," Dad replied.

When finished writing, the Captain handed the papers to Dad and said, "Look them over and see if everything is correct."

Dad looked them over, nodded his approval, signed them, took his physical, and he was in the army.

After Dad had finished basic training, he was sent to Europe with the occupation forces. He was sent to Antwerp, Belgium. From there he went deep into the heart of Germany. He absolutely loved the country and the people. All of his life he spoke well of them and wished them the best. He always followed what was going on in Europe, and for the rest of the world for that matter, but especially Germany.

When the war was over and Dad was being sent into Germany, his two older brothers were on their way back to the States, waiting in Germany for troop movement. Dad and both of his brothers were in the same city at the same time. None of them had any idea the others were there. As they came back to the States, they all lost track of each other for years. Many years after they had all returned, and two years before my Dad's older brother died, the three brothers got together. It was then they learned how close they had been when they were all in Germany - yet missed each other. The last time together, they had a good visit. It was their only time to compare the scars of war and life.

My Roots

My parents started their married life in northern New Mexico. My sister was older. I was the second child, and my parents named me Billy. Dad was William. Mother didn't much like that name for a girl, but she gave into the wishes of my father. She often said, "If that name is good enough for your father and for his country, I suppose it is a good enough name for a girl." So I officially became Billy.

I was born near the end of the great depression. My sister was five years old when my mother, a small, frail woman went to stay with Grandma, so she would have help when I was born. Grandma lived near Durango, in southwestern Colorado.

At that time Durango, and all the small towns around there, were busy little hamlets hidden away in the rough, wild Rocky Mountains. The area was a pristine, untouched, breathtaking wilderness. When I was a child it was pure, and very beautiful. An old train ran down the river's edge, and it gave you the thrill of your life. It roared down the narrow-gage tracks, throwing red-hot cinders into the air. It was a thrill to hear it clatter along - spewing steam and puffing power. For a child, it was formidable.

After I was born, and Mama was back on her feet, we went back home to the small logging town in the Jemez Mountains, in New Mexico to live with Dad and Sis. We lived in an area just as rugged as Colorado. Our cabin was located in the high mountains. There were huge rocks, some as smooth as glass, formed from black volcanic action, with others being as sharp and jagged as razors. There were miles of towering pines, small singing creeks, waiting to be tested by small feet, and full of rainbow trout. The entire area was plush with wildlife, which roamed at will.

Dad's job was with the railroad. He was the sweating, fireman feeding the steam engine as it slowly moved up and down the steep, treacherous mountains to the closest town eighty miles away. Every few days a train load of freshly harvested logs left our camp.

The mountains were peaceful, with a living silence, broken only by the axe of the loggers, the neigh of the big work horses, the crash of falling trees, and the whistle of the train. It was a good time for our family and for

the other workers living in the mountains. It was a free, hard-working, clean life. There were few people living there, and they worked together, they shared good and bad times, and they played together. They became like a family. They loved and trusted each other, and they all looked out for each other.

Memories of Mama

Although Mama seemed big to me, I always knew she was small physically. I don't think she ever weighed more than ninety pounds. She was small boned, and if she really stretched, she might be called five feet tall. She had lustrous, black hair, one blue eye and one brown eye. She had been blinded in one eye when she was a child – two years old.   Even though she had a small build, she had the heart of a lion. She was energetic, quick, and always clear minded.

One day, when I was little, she was outside doing the wash. She boiled the work clothes in a big, outdoor pot over an open fire. Then she picked them out with a sturdy stick, dropped them onto the washboard in the scrub-tub, and rubbed them until clean. Then she dropped them in the rinse water, wrung them out, and hung them on the clothes line to dry.

When she started washing, she had set me on the steps and told me to play right there, which of course, being young and curious, I did not. I saw the big work horses pulling logs, and just walked over to them. When mother looked up to check on me, I was gone. Then she saw me walking right under the feet of one of the horses, patting it on the leg. She dropped everything and ran toward me. Before she got close, she slowed to a casual walk, talked to the horses, reached down, picked me up, and briskly walked to the cabin steps. She quietly sat there for a few minutes. When she had regained her composure, she took my hand and started talking.

"Honey, you do like the horses don't you?"

I nodded my head up and down.

She continued, "I can see that you do, but what you need to remember is that when I tell you to do something it is very important that you do as I tell you. I know the horses are pretty, and they are nice, but they are very big, and very strong. They can hurt you even when they don't mean too – and that could be a very big "ouch." There are also other things around that can hurt you. There are bears, and other animals, so it is important that I know where you are all the time. Now, will you remember that and stay near me when you are outside playing?"

Again, I nodded.

She went on, "Now, if you forget and leave me again, you will have to stay inside with your sister."

That I really did understand. I already knew that I didn't want to stay inside with my big sister. She was so bossy. She would always tell me what to do, and some times she even made me sit on the bench. I didn't like that one bit.

Mama asked again, "Are you sure you understand me?"

I nodded my head again, but this lesson would come back to haunt me more than once.

She smiled, picked me up and hugged me, and went on about her work.

My Parents

I have many fond memories of my parents. I never remember when I was not aware that my Dad adored Mama. I knew he truly loved her. It always gave me pleasure when I remembered them talking about when they got married.

Dad's friend was best man for them and he had a car. He drove my parents, and the maid of honor, to Taos for the wedding. Every time they talked about it, they laughed, but it probably wasn't all that funny when it was happening.

They were married in the summer, when the weather was usually good, but the day my parents married, it was pouring rain. The roads were all dirt, and quite rough, with high ruts, and driving was difficult, especially through the mud.

Mama laughed when she talked about it, and said, "Bill, remember how we drove down the hills, jumped out and pushed the car up the next hill, and then of all things, just before we got to Taos – remember how it rained? Can you believe that? It hardly ever rains in August. Oh my, what a mess we were when we finally got there!"

Then Dad would laugh, and we knew it was also a good memory for him.

They were a beautiful couple. When we lived in the mountains, there would be a dance every Saturday night at the mess hall, and everyone went.

I remember sitting on the bed watching Mama and Dad getting ready to go, both wearing their best clothes, spotless shoes, and always laughing. When they danced, you saw no one else on the dance floor. They danced so gracefully, and moved as if they were one. All eyes were on that handsome couple.

Mama, like the other women, always took food to the dance. There would be cold food inside, and hot food outside on the open fire, and always a big pot of coffee. Everyone would dance, talk, sing, and eat. We all had such a good time. It would be an all night party. When us kids got tired, we would lay down on coats, on the long tables, go to sleep, and wake up the next morning in our beds.

Billy From Scratch

My Dad was of English ancestry. He was tall by this time – six feet one, with curly hair, which he just detested. He would always slick it down as much as possible and flop his *Stetson* hat on his head every time he walked out of the door. I never remember him outside without his hat. Even when he took me fishing, which he often did, he wore his old hat. I've never thought of him any other way. He was very careful in his dress, especially with his shoes and hats. Even when his things got old and worn, they were still clean as a whistle and polished.

Dad's family settled in America, in New England, in the sixteen hundreds. Some of them moved to New Hampshire in 1767. After some time Dad's family split up, with some moving to Mississippi and others to Colorado. My grandfather was born in Meridian, Mississippi, and when he was older, he moved to the West, and my Dad was born in Colorado.

Mama's family also came from England. My grandmother was born in London. She was eight years old when she came to American on an ungainly, wooden ship. It must have been terrible for her, and she would never go on the water again. Every time I was around her she talked about that dreadful trip. I don't know when my mother's family moved to Colorado, however, that was where my mother and my father met.

My parents were married when my father was actually twenty-one, and my mother twenty. She would always tease him because for one month, they were the same age, although his army papers did not show that. Like most happily married couples, they had their little private jokes that they laughed about – his age being one of them. The question was - what age was he? Mama always chuckled and said, "Old!"

Whatever the circumstances, they were happy. You could see it in their faces and in their actions.

Chapter 2

Porter

The early years in the logging town of Porter were good for our family. Our lives were like that of many Americans at that time. The great depression was upon us. Times were hard. No one had very much in the line of money or material things. There was no help of any kind from the government. The only help at all came from close friends and neighbors, and they could offer very little. We were fortunate. Dad still had steady work.

We lived eighty miles from the nearest town. Our logging camp of Porter had no doctors, a one-room country school, and only the company store, which was stocked once a month by way of trucks. We also had a bunk house for the young, single men, a mess hall, and the buildings used for logging and the railroad.

At our house we usually had food. There was an abundance of wild, fresh meat, especially venison, of which we ate a lot. We also had fish in the summer; however, Dad did not eat fish so they gave most of it away.

Mama would buy flour in fifty pound cloth sacks. When the flour was used, the sacks were washed and our clothes were made from them. Mama had an old peddle, sewing machine, which she kept running a great deal of the time. The flour sacks came in pretty prints, which made wonderful dish-towels, pajamas, dresses, and underclothes.

My sister and I entertained ourselves much of the time. We thrived through healthy neglect although we always knew that we were supposed to stay close to camp. We climbed trees, waded in the cold, icy streams, played games we invented, and most of the time we were free to do pretty much as we pleased.

At night we always had supper together. That was a hard, fast rule. It was an occasion for eating, but also an opportunity for conversation. We didn't know it at the time, but a lot of our education came from those talks. We talked about everything, but it was always understood that what was said at the table, remained at the table – it was private.

After supper and the dishes were done, Mama would sew, or often mend socks. Most of the time, Dad would read aloud to us. He read all kinds of books. We would stretch out on the floor, on a big bear rug, occasionally looking into the bear's mouth, and feeling his teeth, all the time listening to the story until bedtime. One night a week, we were allowed to listen to the radio for sometimes as long as an hour. We loved to listen to *Fibber McGee and Molly*, and always laughed through *Amos 'n Andy*. Sometimes we would just sing songs. Sis and I would sing along with anything, and sometimes even make up silly words or songs of our own.

It seemed to me that Mama was always the one that people turned to if they had any problems. As I remember she was the accepted *Medicine Man* in our area. She always kept emergency supplies, and knew how to use things when they were needed by someone. She used a lot of herbs, most of which she collected and dried during the summer.

She had a remedy for colds, pneumonia, coughs, cramps, fever, burns, weak bones, headaches, and one for *summer complaint*, and so many more. She was quite knowledgeable. She used many old time remedies. I think she learned a lot of them from her mother, but she also learned some of them from the local Indians. She was always friendly with the Indians and they seemed to accept my mother as one of their own, which was an unusual thing.

Mama was also quite inventive with food. She preserved her own dried beans, corn, and carrots – different fruits. She made her own relishes, pickles, and mince meat. She canned, dried, and preserved food in all known ways for that time. She used many old, time-tested recipes. Here is one of her recipes.

"Mince Meat pie:

2 cups finely-chopped lean beef

4 cups finely-chopped tart apples

2 cups chopped raisins

2 cups currants

1 cup of finely-chopped citron

2 tsp salt

1 tbsp nutmeg

1 cup suet, chopped

2 cups granulated sugar

1 cup strong coffee or cider

1 tbsp ground cloves

1 tbsp cinnamon

1 cup meat stock

Use lean meat, if available, and cook until tender. Cool in the liquid, and then put the meat through a chopper. Put apples, raisins, currants, citron, salt, nutmeg, and suet through the chopper also. Add the remainder of the ingredients together in the order named, and mix well. Simmer slowly for an hour. Bottle the mixture while hot, wipe top

11

of jar, and seal. Process the filled jars in a pressure cooker immediately. This recipe makes about 5 pints."

I have vivid memories of those pies. We usually had mince meat and pumpkin pie for holidays. Now that I look back at this recipe, I have often wondered how one person can accomplish so much with so little. I do remember Mama also using venison in this mince pie recipe instead of beef. However she did it, her cooking was wonderful. As I said, Mama always made the most of what she had.

She also made a number of mixes. They saved her a lot of time. This is another one from her cookbook. I also liked this one.

"Pancake Mix

> *6 cups flour*
>
> *8 tbsp sugar*
>
> *6 rounding tbsp baking powder*
>
> *3 tsp salt*
>
> *8 tbsp lard*
>
> *4 tbsp dried eggs*
>
> *¼ cup of dried milk*

Mix well. Store in cool place in covered container. Take out amount you want, add enough water to make correct consistency. Stir as little as possible. Cook on hot grill, and serve with butter and syrup."

We ate these often, and enjoyed them along with many other home-made things, such as: lemon pie, raisin pie, corn bread, warm gingerbread with whipped cream, when cream was available, which was not often. We also had baked custard, devil's food cake, cornmeal griddle cakes, sugar cookies, fig pudding, and whatever was available.

My parents were always clever. I remember one Thanksgiving. We were having company that we had not seen for a long time – an aunt and uncle - so this was a special time. We had venison, but no turkey.

Mama said, "Fine. No problem, we'll have venison."

Dad said, "I think maybe we could have a turkey. I saw some nice ones the other day. They have been pecking around behind the cabin."

The following day Dad made a path of shelled corn from the cabin up into the hills behind us. He put a trap under the edge of the cabin porch, and then waited. Sure enough, soon a big turkey started picking up that corn and followed it right into the trap. Dad caught the turkey, killed and cleaned it. We had turkey and venison for Thanksgiving.

Dinner was great. My sister had a beautiful little set of blue and white China dishes. Grandmother had given them to my sister because she was the oldest. The dishes came from England.

Mama put a pretty little table cloth on the big trunk, and Sis and I got to eat on the *special table* for Thanksgiving. We sat on the little benches that Dad had made for us. Mama had made a pretty cushion for each seat. We had a wonderful time. It was a very special occasion for us.

The Roundhouse

The biggest building in camp was the roundhouse. It was built with a turntable in the center, which was used to turn the train around, and it was also used when repairs were required on the flatcars. The train was essential and was only used to take logs to the closest town, past the Indian pueblo, and away from the mountains. The roundhouse was always a big, scary place to me. I was inside only once with Dad, and I never wanted to go again. The train was big and noisy and steam always seemed to spew from the engine.

One night neither the train, nor the roundhouse, was on my mind as Sis and I went to bed at the usual time. Dad had just finished reading to us, and we talked a little while about the story, and soon we were both fast asleep.

I awoke with a start. I saw strange shadows on the walls, and I thought I heard shouting. Then I realized that Sis was out of bed and talking with Mama. I slipped out of bed and went to join them.

Mama turned to me, and she looked tired. She held out her arms, and I slipped in close to her, feeling something was dreadfully wrong.

"What's the matter, Mama? Where is Daddy?"

"It is the train, Honey, there is a bad fire and your Dad is helping. The fire is at the roundhouse. They got the engine out, but it doesn't look like they will save the building. I think we will all be lucky if they can just keep the fire from spreading."

"Can we watch, Mama?" I asked.

"Yes, you can if you want to, but you stay right here with your sister, and don't go outside. I'm going to make some coffee and sandwiches for the men. Remember to stay inside."

Sis reached over, and touched my hand. "Don't worry. You do not need to be afraid," she said.

I moved nearer to my sister. I had never felt so close to her as at that moment. I knew no matter what, she would always be there for me through thick or thin. We formed a bond that night, standing side by side, looking out the window, watching the fire with apprehension. I saw my sister in a new and different way. There was nothing to do to save the roundhouse. It was gone, but a new connection was born, one that would never be broken. My sister and I would always be close.

The fire was just about out when Dad finally came home, he was tired and dirty. He smelled of smoke and fire. He washed and then sat at the table talking with Mama, and although by this time we had gone back to bed, we could hear them talking.

"Bill, what is this going to do with the logging business?" Mama asked.

"I don't know. We'll just have to wait and see. We might have a job, but things are pretty rough right now, so I just don't know. I really don't expect them to rebuild the roundhouse," he said, half thinking to himself.

Then Dad patted Mama on the hand, smiled at her, and said, "Now we are not going to worry about the job until we know what happens. We just have to believe that everything is going to be all right. This won't be the first storm we've weathered."

Even though I was young, I felt a change in the air – something was happening, and I didn't understand it, but I knew I didn't like it either. I continued to go fishing with Dad, and he still laughed and told me stories, but somehow I knew there was a difference. Once in a while, I would notice a worried look pass over his face. Then he would see me looking at him, smile and talk about something he knew I was interested in.

There was still work in the logging woods, but the depression was hurting more and more people, and the fire did not help where we lived. At our house, we were still eating, even though food was sometimes more scarce than it had been, and it turned to more and more plain food, mainly venison or other wild things, but at least we were not going hungry. Although work became less and less, we continued to eat. There was a lot of wild food available if you could find it, or kill it.

Brownie

One day Sis and I had a big surprise. Dad came home with a present for us. Wrapped in his arms was a beautiful, little baby bear. Dad said that a baby bear would be called a cub. He didn't hand him to us right away. First he let us pet him, but next came the lesson.

"Now kids," he said, "this is a real live, baby animal. It is wild. The only reason you are getting it is because Sam Wilson had to kill its' mother. Sam had startled the mother bear, when he came upon her unexpectedly, and she had attacked him so he had no choice. As soon as he saw her he stood very quiet, and talked to her in a moderate voice, but in the end he had to shoot her. She would not stop the attack."

Dad said, "There is one other thing you both must understand and agree too. When this bear gets to a certain age, you must give it up. Then it will have to go to the zoo, or some animal reserve. You see even though it is playful now, it is wild, and always will be wild. When animals get older, they often become dangerous. And one more thing, you two will be responsible for feeding and taking care of him. If I see your mother doing it one time, the bear is gone. Now - do you want it?"

Well, of course, we wanted it. We were both elated. Dad built Brownie a nice home, and we played with that lovely, little bear every day. Oh how we loved him! He was a blackish, brown, and he was just like a little dog. He would bite on our fingers, nuzzle us, run away and come back, and when he got tired, he would snuggle up to us and go to sleep. We simply loved him, and were delighted with him. We played with our little bear constantly, and we called him Brownie.

Then one day a bad thing happened. We had played with Brownie for quite a while. We stopped and ran into the cabin for something. The bear still wanted to play I guess, and went to play with the horses. When we came back outside, he was patting one of the big work horses on the back leg, and the horse kicked. It killed Brownie instantly. What a sad day that was for Sis, and for me. We had a full funeral, wild flowers, and a lot of crying. It was my first feel of death.

After we buried our little bear, I was sitting on the back steps crying. Mama came and sat down beside me, slipping her arm around me.

"Honey," she said, "I know this is a hurtful thing for you, and for your sister, but these things just happen."

"But Dad told us it was our job to take care of him, and we went into the house. If we had put Brownie in his house and locked the door, he wouldn't have gone to play with the horses, and he wouldn't be dead. He would have stayed with us. It was our fault, Mama. We shouldn't have left him outside alone."

"Well, maybe not," she answered, "but sometimes, no matter what we do, or don't do, things happen. Some things we have no control over. We are just human. We have to do the very best we can. And we all know that neither of you expected anything bad to happen to Brownie in just the few minutes you ran into the house. Isn't that true?"

"Yes Mama," I said, "but I don't like dead."

"Well, Honey, all I know is that Brownie is dead, and he will never be here for you and your sister to play with again. You will have to accept that he is gone. You see, everything that is alive will in time die. When animals, and even when people, are born, we know that in time they will die. That is true for everything. Does that still scare you?"

"Yes, Mama," I answered.

"Well, little one, don't be afraid of that. We have no control over when we are born, or when we die. If we are going to worry about anything, then let us worry about something that we can do something about. It might help, if you just think about Brownie being with his mother. See him as being happy, and know that you and your sister did the best job that you knew how to do. Can you do that?"

I shook my head up and down, and said, "I'll try Mama." However, I still felt empty, with an ache in my stomach. I knew we were going to miss Brownie. I also knew it really was our fault.

The Meadow

"Tomorrow your Dad is going fishing. I don't suppose you want to go with him," Mama said.

"Yes I do!" I beamed.

"Sis and I are going to bake while you two are fishing. We might have something good for you when you get back."

She smiled and added, "One other thing, remind your Dad that he has something to show you."

"What is it, Mama? Tell me, please."

"Oh no, I can't tell you now. That would spoil your Dad's surprise. You just think about it before you go to sleep tonight. Think of something very beautiful, and very nice." She kissed me on the forehead, and walked back to the stove.

It was early morning as Dad and I reached the cool, quick creek. We quietly fished the deeper holes, catching a few nice rainbow trout. It was always a quiet time when we fished.

Dad said, "When you trout fish, you need to cast your line into the quiet, deep holes where the fish like to hide. If you talk or move around much, you will scare them, and they won't bite."

I loved fishing. I liked the peacefulness of it, and also the quiet time for thinking. I also liked the time spent with my Dad.

Some time before I felt my usual hunger pains, Dad said, "Come on, Sis, pack up your gear. We are going for a walk." I knew immediately this was the surprise Mama had talked about.

"Where are we going, Dad?" I asked.

"Just come on, you'll see," he answered.

We packed up, threw our gear over our shoulders, and started slowly climbing uphill through the brush and the thick, tall pines. We would walk for awhile, then rest.

Finally we reached the top of the ridge, and for the first time in my life, I couldn't say a word. I simply stood and looked at the wonderful view in front of me. It was the most amazing thing I have ever seen. My eyes feasted on the cone of an ancient volcano. It was miles wide. In the center spread a lush meadow with a small stream dividing it, and an old, log barn. The grass was high. All through the entire meadow, there were yellow and purple flowers in full bloom. Here and there was a pretty, red, Indian paintbrush, and there were little groups of small, wild white daisies – the kind we always put on our mud cakes as decoration. It was the most beautiful sight I had ever seen, and the smell was lovely. I stood quietly, taking it all in, until the dam broke within me, followed by a torrent of wonder, and awe. I was overwhelmed with happiness. I laughed, and ran amok, in circles amid the flowers, finally flinging myself down upon the sweet smelling earth. As I looked up, I saw beautiful blue sky, with white fluffy clouds, and a sea of yellow and purple above me. I lay there for some time not wanting to break the wonderful spell of fascination.

Finally Dad came laughing and picked me up, and set me on a high fallen log. He sat down beside me and opened our lunch bag. He started talking as he handed me a peanut butter and jelly sandwich.

"Sis," he said, "you may not know it yet, but you are the richest girl in the world. What can you ever have that is worth more than what you have seen today? You cannot put a price on it. Sis, this is worth more than anything you can ever buy. You own what you have seen here today. It is like education. Once you have it, no one, nor anything, can ever steal it from you. What is in your head will always be yours."

He continued, "Tomorrow we will come back here for a picnic. We will bring your mother and your sister. You can do what you want, but if I were you, I would not take this surprise away from her. Let's let her see it for herself. OK?"

I understood immediately, and said, *"Okey-doke.* I won't tell her a word. She is really going to be surprised, and I know she will love it as much as I do. She will be so happy, Dad."

We finished our lunch, took another look at the flowers, and then slowly walked home. The sun was starting to go down, and the mountains in the distance turned a soft, mellow pink. The air smelled fresh, with a touch of sweetness from the blooming flowers. My heart was dancing.

When we got home there were fresh baked, oatmeal cookies, just as Mama had promised. She even let us have one before supper if we promised to clean our plates at supper.

As we ate, I could not help but smile at Dad because of our secret surprise for Sis. Mama frowned at us, but she could not help but smile too.

Chapter 3

Fire, Fire – Everywhere!

After the family picnic, times remained relatively good for us. We fared better than many families, but the following year things quickly changed. Soon hard times were upon us with a vengeance.

It was early in the morning of a windy, cool day, when the town emergency bell started violently ringing. It rang and rang. People dropped everything and ran to the mess hall.

A few minutes earlier, I had seen the forest ranger come into camp and go directly to the office of the boss. Now the two men stood before us at the mess hall, and the boss started talking.

"Folks, we have a grave emergency on our hands." Nodding his head toward the ranger, he continued, "I'll let Jerry tell you about it."

"Friends," said Jerry, "I want to get right to the point here because time is not on our side. We have a forest fire over on the next ridge. With this wind, it could be here in no time. Now you all know what the plan is in case of a fire of this kind. I will be here to help as long as it takes, so let's just break this up and everyone get busy. I will not say not to worry, because there is a lot to worry about, but you all know what needs to be done and how to do it. This is a full alert, so let's go!"

Dad turned to mother and said, "Well honey, you know the ropes. The evacuation trucks will be here at the mess hall, ready if they are needed. Just collect what you absolutely need, and try to stay together. If you do have to leave, don't wait for me. We will fight this as long as we have to, and I will find you when it is all over."

He quickly kissed her on the cheek, patted us kids on the top of our heads, and he was gone.

The camp was a mad house all day. Trucks gassed up, and rolled up to the mess hall ready to evacuate the entire camp. First aid supplies were laid out. Big pots of coffee were made, hot and ready for tired workers. Food was prepared, but before these things were all done, we could see the glow of the oncoming fire nibbling at the top of the ridge. A touch of queasiness made me weak.

Sis and I stood inside the cabin, by the window, watching the far away glow. Shortly our eyes would return to the busy beehive of the camp. Every available man and woman was fighting the fire in some way, each with the hope of stopping it before it consumed everything.

All this activity took my mind back to something Dad had told us a long time ago. All of my life, Dad had always talked to us about everything, and he made a point of talking about things that we really needed to know to survive. He had talked to us at different times about fires completely out of control. Sometimes they were horrid. People were burned alive, houses, animals, whole towns sometimes. He had told us, if you are ever caught in one, sometimes you can save yourself if you are close to water, or if there are caves close, or any kind of deep underground shelter.

He told us about a forest ranger that was caught in a fire, and knew he had no way of escape. All he had was a shovel, and a heavy fire-cover with him. He found the clearest spot, and furiously dug a trench, threw himself down into the bottom, and quickly covered his body with the cover, and as much dirt as he could pull upon him. When the fire was close, he pulled the cover, with more dirt, over his face. He worked his arms underneath to give himself as much air as possible, and waited.

Fortunately, the fire was traveling fast and quickly passed over him before he succumbed. He was later found, frightened to death, and burned some around his hands and face, but his quick thinking had saved his life.

Dad said that he never gave up being a forest ranger, and that he lived to be an old man. I could tell the way that my Dad talked about him, that he respected him. He had told us that he was not only a smart man, but he was a brave man, one you could always depend on to do the right thing.

The rumble and conflagration of the fire brought me back to our present danger. Again my stomach seemed to turn. Soon there were tears running down my cheeks, and I wondered when we would get into the trucks and go away from this awful, fiendish monster. Then Sis came to stand by me at the window. "Don't be afraid," she said. "Dad and the men will get the fire stopped, but if they don't we will leave with the trucks when it is time."

"How can we go and leave without Dad?" I asked.

"We have to because that is what Dad said," she answered. "He has to believe that we are doing what he told us to do, because that is the safest thing to do, and besides, it is up to us to take care of Mama."

"Mama," I questioned. "Why do we have to take care of Mama? She always takes care of us."

"Well, silly goose, don't you know that Mama is not well?"
She looked straight at me, questioning if I had any brains or not. Then she asked, "When you and Dad go fishing, why do you think I always stay with Mama?"

"I don't know."

"Well, it is because Mama has a very bad heart. That is why I stay with her so much, and help her when I can. It wouldn't hurt you to help her a little bit more either."

"What am I suppose to do? I clean the lamps. I help Dad pile the wood. Sometimes, I even dry the dishes."

"That's true," she said, looking me straight in the eye. "You do those things, but just keep in mind that the more we help her the better it is. And don't you dare tell her that you know about this. She wouldn't like it if she knew I told you. I am worried about her with this fire though. I know she is concerned about Dad, and she is worried about us, so let's do as much as we can to help. Another thing – don't cry!"

Later in the day Mama rested for awhile. Then our neighbor, Mrs. Adams, came to our door and asked for her. Mama had already heard her, and was up immediately.

"Florence, Jim Wilson was hurt. They brought him in and he is at the mess hall. Can you come?"

"Certainly," Mama answered. She grabbed her bag of herbs, medicines, and supplies.

She turned to us and said, "I don't know how long I will be gone. If things get worse, you can come to the mess hall, but be careful and watch for trucks and things moving. If you have to come, stay together and hold hands. I'll be back as soon as I can."

She opened the door, then turned back to us, "Remember, I'm depending on you. I can see you from the mess hall, and I'll keep an eye out. You do the same."

Looking at Sis, she said, "Take care of your little sister now." Then she was gone.

I was really scared when she left, first Dad and then Mama. I held my sister's hand for dear life, but I didn't cry. It seemed forever before Mama came back. She looked tired, and she had soot smudges on her.

She said, "I think Jim is going to be just fine. I think it was mainly over-exertion. His wife is with him now. After some more fluids and some rest, he will be as good as new."

It was still day, but dark from the smoke, and Mama said, "Now let's get you girls something to eat, then maybe you better rest for awhile."

We did go to sleep, but when I woke up, I knew it was night, even though it was light in the room, and there was a strange flickering

of reds and orange dancing on the walls and furniture. Then that awful, unsettled feeling hit my stomach again as I remembered the fire coming closer. I did not say it out loud, but I asked myself, "How can Dad leave us alone? I'm so afraid."

I don't think Mama had even gone to bed. When Sis woke up, we all went out, sat on the back porch, and watched the fire. It seemed so close - almost upon us. There are no words to describe it. It smelled horrendous - the smoke and burning animals. The noise tore right through you like a knife. It was so loud. There were the sounds of dynamite, sounds of the working equipment, and worst of all, the noise of the fire itself. The sound continued to explode all around, and the burn stink stayed in your nose and throat. Fear simply overwhelmed us.

Mama stood up and said, "It is like looking directly into hell. Come on inside. You've both seen enough."

"Is it time to leave, Mama?" I asked.

"No, not yet, Honey. The men are watching very closely though, and we may need to go. If they ring the bell, then we will go. Remember keep your things together so we are ready, and when we go, don't go back for anything," she said. "Now I think it is time for some hot chocolate, and a little something to eat."

Food did not taste good. We all ate very little, and then Mama cleaned up and said, "You two go rest for a while. Try to sleep. Talk about nice things, and you won't need to worry either. I'll be awake, and I will watch." She kissed us both as we made our way back to bed, and we watched her as she settled into her old, handmade, wooden rocking chair by the window. Sis and I talked for a long time, but after awhile we both were sleeping again.

It seemed like the fire lasted for ever, but it was just a few days before the fire started dying down enough to make the men feel they just about had it under control. Then one morning I woke up and knew Dad was home. I jumped out of bed and ran to Mama. She put her finger to her mouth and said, "Shush, your Dad is sleeping. He is very tired, and we want him to sleep as long as he needs to."

27

"OK, Mama, I'll be quiet."

"It won't be long now, and he will be up. While he is sleeping, let's have a bite to eat and then go wash his stinky clothes. He took a bath when he got home, but those clothes are terrible."

Sis got up and after we finished eating, we went outside. The fire had died-down considerably since we all saw it last. I knew that was why Dad had come home, but I also knew he would probably go back.

We boiled water and Mama washed his clothes. Sis rinsed them and wrung them out. We both hung them up to dry. By the time we had finished, Dad was up and he was hungry. Mama made eggs, potatoes, and bacon for him. When he was finished, he sat on the porch, and drank black coffee.

Looking at the fire Dad said, "Well I think we have just about licked her. She was a tough one. Lucky no one was seriously hurt, and it didn't take the camp. It sure did burn a lot of good lumber though."

"Fires are bad, Dad. I don't like them," I said.

Sis nodded her head in agreement.

Dad smiled, but did not answer instantaneously. Finally he said, "Well, they are, but they are not. Think about it like this. Fires certainly are scary when they get out of hand, but just think of how good they are."

"What do you mean, Dad?" Sis asked.

Ask yourself, "How would I have had the wonderful breakfast this morning without fire? How would you girls, and your Mama, have gotten my dirty clothes clean without water heated by fire? How could we live here in the mountains, in the cold winters, without fire? You see fire is not good, nor is it bad. It is just fire. What is important is the way we use it. Fire is a tool. It keeps us warm, it cooks our food, and it helps us make tools. Those are all good things."

Dad continued, "Now the bad thing is that sometimes people become careless with fire, not only fire, but with a lot of things. For example, if you go out camping and do not thoroughly put your fire out, that can cause a forest fire, and you know how scary and dangerous that is. Sometimes people do not think and they throw cigarettes out of their car window, and that can start a fire. You see, in both cases, these people did not use fire carefully. Do you see the difference?"

"Yeah," said Sis. "Why do people do that, Dad?"

"Mainly it is because some people just don't think. It's usually not that they are unkind, or that they want to hurt someone, it's just that they do things without thinking how it affects other people."

He thought for a few minutes, and then he went on, "I think what we all need to remember is that whatever we do usually influences someone else - sometimes in ways we may never even think of. We may never even know it, but any one of us may be a model for someone. So the important thing is, whenever you do anything, ask yourself if you are being a good role model."

Mama came out from the house and sat with us. She said, "Bill, you're getting a little heavy for these kids. They will learn these things when it is time."

"Well, honey, there is no better time than right now. They have just seen what other people's carelessness can do. It kept these girls on edge for a long time, and it put us all in danger."

Then Dad grinned, and went on, "Remember when we read the book about Aristotle?" Then he looked directly at us, and waited a few minutes. "Remember?" he asked again.

Sis said, "Sure, I remember. He was the funny man in the book that wore the strange shoes and wore white sheets."

"That's the one. He was a very smart Greek that lived a long time ago. He was the man that said that the four main elements of life are air, water, fire and earth. These were the elements our world was made from – and we cannot live without any of these. See, if any of these were missing, there would be no world. What he was talking about was that these are our four most important tools in order for all things to live on earth. I can't emphasize how important it is for us to take care of them all."

"Now, if you think about that in that way- can you see how this forest fire might not have happened if people had been responsible with only one of those tools – the tool of fire?"

We both nodded our heads. Then we knew that fire was not bad at all. It is just the way you use it – like Dad said.

Dad rubbed our heads, and stood up. "I better get back to the fire." he said. "It is time for someone else to get a break."

He gave Mama a peck on the cheek and said, "We have pretty much isolated this fire, and the backfires worked well, but you can never tell when the wind will come up. We will have to watch those big, burning logs, and the flying sparks for some time. We have to make sure it is completely out. I'll be home as soon as I can."

Chapter 4

The Poker Game

After the roundhouse burned, and the forest fire was over, everyone in camp concentrated on getting back to normal. The fires left a terrible mess, but we did everything possible to clean up. Both fires had left major damage, both to the logging business, and the camp itself. It would take years for the trees to grow, and the wild life to return. Logging went on, but there was a definite change in the air, not only in the mountains, but through the entire country. Fire was not the only scoundrel. Unemployment, hunger and hopelessness were showing up everywhere. People were hurting. The United States was deep into the *Great Depression.*

One night I woke up. I heard voices. I knew what it was. I had heard it before. The blanket was pulled shut, thus making our sleeping area closed off, but I could hear very well.

I recognized Dad's voice first. "Well John, are you glued to those cards. Are you going to play or not?"

John Baker was my Dad's best friend. Dad was a big man by this time, but not nearly as big as John. He was a bear of a man, and a good logger. He had a wonderful disposition. He always laughed a lot. I really liked him. He had a pretty, bright wife, three boys, and two girls. The youngest girl was my age, and they called her *Little John.*

31

John was from another state, but had known my Dad for years. One day I asked Dad how he ever became friends with Uncle John. Uncle John had told us we could call him uncle because we were just like his kids.

Dad told me, "John was working here when I came. He is a good man. He has good principles, takes care of his family, and does his work. He is fair and honest. He lives a good life. I like the man. He is made of all the right stuff." I knew that Dad thought the world of him.

Suddenly Matt Hatfield's voice brought me back to the conversation that woke me up. Matt was another regular card player. He was also a logger, young, big and dark. I thought he was about the best looking man I ever saw. I told Mama that I was going to marry him.

Dad heard what I had said. He just threw back his head and laughed. "Sis, you don't want to marry a bootlegger."

I didn't know what that meant for a long time, but I knew Matt always had more money than anyone I ever knew. When Dad was driving an old junk car, Matt had a new, spiffy car. I remember when Mama saw him coming, she always frowned. I didn't think she approved of him for some reason.

Matt was married to a very pretty woman. She always wore her hair in a pageboy, and it shined like a million dollars. She always dressed real nice too. I liked her a lot. They didn't have any children though – no one to play with.

I heard Matt ask Pedro if he wanted another drink.

"*Si*," said Pedro Martinez. Pedro was another good friend of my Dad, and a regular card player. He was the company mechanic, and Dad said he always did a good job. That seemed to be important to Dad – the measure of a person. Pedro was a small, frail looking man, Mexican and part Indian. He had lost his wife many years ago to tuberculosis. He had one son that had moved to California a few years back, and he had one daughter. She lived down state somewhere, with her own family. Pedro had lived alone since they all left. He was always very pleasant, but he seemed to be lonely. Dad never forgot to ask him over when they played cards, and Mama would invite him over to eat with us quite often.

Matt handed the bottle to Pedro, and he took a drink and passed it around.

Dad looked at Matt and said, "You better watch your step, Son. Even though prohibition has been repealed, the law can still get you. You know we have a lot of new laws now, and we see those federal boys around here pretty often."

Matt laughed and said, "Hell, don't matter how much work there is, the liquor business is always good. I *ain't* heard tell of men not drinking - work or no work. Don't worry. They will never get me, besides I never hurt *nothin'*. I don't make no rot-gut whiskey. You know things are getting worse right along. Everybody knows a man needs some income. Besides narry a man ever said that I don't try to abide by the Good Book. My thinking is, it is gonna be up to us if we sink or swim. Even if all of Roosevelt's programs work, it'll be a good while for it to work down to us."

John agreed and said, "You can't argue with that. I never thought that there would be a lack of work here in the woods. We use wood for everything. Without wood, how are we going to build anything? Then we need paper. Everything is going to paper."

Pedro chimed in, "I know a lot of people have big trouble since the banks closed in '29. Everybody is bad off. No money. Some got sick, like my wife. Some lose kids - many die. Things get better sometimes maybe, but bad now."

Matt asked, "What do you think of this Roosevelt *feller*? What's that they call his new government programs? I think they call it the New Deal. "

John frowned and answered, "Yeah, but I don't know. He makes a lot of promises, but talk is cheap. Hoover talked good too. He promised to get the waste out of government. He talked about cutting the cost of government. He didn't do either one. Some say it was his fault that the stock market crashed. Hell, I would like to see some government official doing something for us working hands. I don't know. Maybe Roosevelt won't do anything. He could just be another one of those rich fellows out to make all he can for his own good. There has been a lot of that."

John looked at Dad, "Well Bill, you read a lot and keep up on things. What do you think of our new president?"

"I see a lot of good in him. When he was Governor of New York, he helped provide cheaper utilities. He also helped the farmers. I know Hoover was working under difficult conditions, but I think Roosevelt has had the whole ball-of-wax dumped into his lap. Right now I hear a lot of talk about developing electric power. There is talk about working down around Tennessee on flood control, and they even say, 'Everyone will have electric power one day.' I don't know about that, but these are hard times, and seem to be getting harder. People are in despair. Hell, people are jumping off of buildings. What we need is real leadership, a president that watches out for us working men. I think Roosevelt might be that man. The working men were the ones that built this country, and the country still needs us. Let's give him a chance. Hell, the man can't even walk. Any man that can beat polio must have something on the ball. I'd say, give him some time and support."

John pushed his chair back, looked around and said, "Well, better save all your pennies *fellers*. I think we are all gonna need them."

With that settled, all three went home, and Dad went to bed.

The After-Math

Time was slipping away. There was less and less work at the logging camp. People were feeling the bite of poverty. Most of the working people had put on a hard front, although they were worried to the core. That year our little school closed.

My parents had decided that Sis would have to attend a private school if she were to get any education. That was a top priority for them. When it was time for school to start, my sister went to a boarding school eighty miles from where we lived in the mountains. It would be her first year away from home, and she would stay the entire school year. Mama sewed and worked all summer getting her ready. For me, and my parents, it was a sad day when we took her to school. I think Sis had mixed feelings. She wanted to go to school, and loved learning, so that aspect she liked. What she did not like was leaving home – especially for such a long time.

The day we left, she looked so beautiful. She was always such a pretty girl anyway, always prettier than I was. That day she looked especially nice – bright eyes, and pretty teeth, straight-cut, dark hair, and she was perfectly groomed. She wore a new dress, primly starched, and ironed. She had on long, white stockings and black Sara Janes.

She would have one uniform, which she would pick up at school. It was a long sleeve, white blouse, and worn with a mid-length, blue jumper. She would wear it all year to school - every time she went to class. She would have to change her clothes as soon as school was over, and put on her play clothes.

We packed the car with Sis's belongings. Mama packed a lunch, which we would eat on the way. Dad filled the canvas water bag that he hung on the front bumper of the car to keep the water cool. Mama threw a couple of pillows and a blanket in the car, and we left on our long drive.

Billy From Scratch

Dad drove, as Mama never learned to drive, and Sis and I sat in the back seat, waving the smoke from Dad's cigar out of the window.

We slowly descended the rough, narrow, dirt roads, keeping to the inside when we reached a curve, thus giving the log trucks enough room to turn on the sharp curves. In one place you could see way down to the bottom of the canyon. There was an old truck that had gone over the edge. It had been there for many years, but there was still enough red paint showing to see the color.

There were times when we would meet a logging truck that would go by us, and it would scare me to death. I would close my eyes until I knew it was past.

Dad pulled off the road at our familiar water stop and we got out and ran up the hill to the ice cold spring. We drank right out of the spring, holding the water in our hands. It always tasted wonderful.

Soon we were back in the car and passing Battleship Rock. When you came up this road from the other direction, the rock right in front of you looked like a ship bearing right down on you. It was grey granite rock that looked exactly like a gigantic sea vessel. About five miles down the road, we came to what Dad called Sulfur Springs. They were hot bathing springs just above the mineral deposit dam that everyone called the Soda Dam. It was a natural dam about 300 feet wide and bridging the river and making a nice, little waterfall. The dam was a beautiful site, with smooth rocks, and soft, mellow colors. There were always people taking pictures; however, the hot springs were hidden further up the hill.

For my family, the springs were the best bath in the world. Not many people knew about them. Usually when we went there, we would be the only people. Once in a while there might be one or two others.

These springs were wonderful. They did smell a little like sulfur, but they were so hot it took some time before you could slip into the water. I always loved going there.

The next thing of interest to me was the Jemez Indian Pueblo. There were always kids playing there, and I would wave to them, and they always waved back. They had goats running around, and sometimes you could smell fresh bread baking in the outside ovens. I liked it.

After passing the pueblo, the ride became tedious, and as I often did along this stretch, I covered up with the blanket and went to sleep until we reached Bernalillo. That would always catch my interest as it was a much bigger place than anything I would usually see. There were schools there, churches, stores, and a lot of people. Dad would often wave and call people by name, but we continued on without stopping.

Finally we reached Albuquerque. We slowly drove down to the Rio Grande River area. This was really big city to us. At last Dad reached the boarding school and we parked.

The school was unbelievable to me. It was a big, square, white, two-story building. There was a wide, brick walk leading to the front door. The school area filled a big space. Along the walk were big cottonwood trees. There was grass and shrubs, and play areas. It was beautiful. I never saw a school like that before.

We got out, carried Sis' things with us, and went inside. The front door opened into a wide entrance area. The floors were wood. They shined like a beautifully finished table. The windows were high with lacy curtains over them. There were benches on one side, and we sat down while Dad went into the office of the head mistress. After a short time she came out, and shook our hands.

She said, "Come with me and I will show you the school." She took Sis by the hand, and we walked through the entire school.

The main floor was offices, school rooms, bathrooms, a large dining room, and off the back of the building was a glass-enclosed porch where students were allowed to play games, read, or study.

Upstairs were sleeping rooms. Each room held two girls. Every room had a double closet and a chest, a study area, and two single beds. Each room had a window with a nice view. Down the hall were bathrooms and showers, and an exercise area. There was also a library, with reading tables and chairs. There were benches covered with big cushions, located in front of the windows, providing a lovely place to read.

When our tour was over, Sis was given her uniform and we helped her take her things to her room and put them away. Then we all hugged and left Sis there for the school year. She never shed a tear. She smiled and waved. I thought she was very brave.

It was the biggest change in her life, and mine as well. It was a long, quiet ride home, and I felt so bad about leaving Sis all alone in the big city. I knew she would do well there, but I also knew she would much rather be going home with us. Then I remembered about Dad telling us how lucky we were to live in the mountains, and how we had riches that couldn't be bought. For the first time I realized exactly what he had been trying to tell me when we saw the flowers in the meadow.

Suddenly I knew, no matter how pretty that school was, no matter what a nice place Sis had to stay, we were the lucky ones. We were going home; however, on the other hand, a new world had opened up for Sis.

As a new life was to start for her, my old life had become rather dull, and I missed her. I was now required to stay closer to the cabin; however, Dad read more and more to Mama and me. There was less work for Dad, and people slowly started leaving the area. Dad still had work, but only a few days a week. Winter was coming on, and the days grew dark and bleak. Soon the snow was heavily falling, and the road became impenetrable. No supply trucks could reach camp, and food soon became scarce. Every day became more of a struggle for existence.

One day Little John came running to our cabin. She was frantic, her hair flying in the wind, and her eyes as big as saucers. She blurted out, "Uncle Bill come quick. My daddy is crazy and he says he is going to kill himself."

"Now, now," Dad said, "does he have a gun out?"

"I don't think so, but I know he has one."

As Dad slipped on his coat, and picked up his hand gun, he said, "Now you just stay right here with Billy and I'll see to your Dad. Don't you fret. Everything is going to be all right."

When Dad got to John and Margaret's cabin, they were both distraught. John was raving, acting like an unbalanced man, while Margaret was frantic.

John stared at Dad and said, "No use to try to talk me out of this. I've made up my mind."

"That's fine," said Dad. "Margaret, why don't you go over and talk to Florence and the girls. John and I have a few things to talk about. Does that suit you, John?"

John looked at Dad with a baffled look on his face, and growled, "Well, I guess so. Go on Margaret."

When Margaret had left, Dad just quietly sat down and didn't say a word for a long while.

John said, "Bill, I've got to do this. I'm in a hell-of-a-mess. We don't even have enough to eat. I can't stand to see my little ones like this. I don't know how this happened, or what more I can do."

"John, we're all in the same boat. We do not have much either, so I know what you're going through. We have talked about this before, and you know what we decided. We will all share what we have."

Dad collected himself, and started talking in a low, calm voice. He said, "John, we've been friends a long time, and I know this is a very stressful time, but let me just ask you: What will happen to Margaret and your kids if you do this? How is the rest of the camp going to survive without you? Winter won't last forever, and we all need you, John. There is another thing, don't you realize that if you do this, it will drop a heavy burden on your wife and kids for as long as they live? Have you really thought this through?"

Dad studied John's face. He looked at Dad quizzically, so Dad knew he had to get John's full attention, and do it quickly, so he continued, "Well John, I guess this is your decision. It is up to you. If you want to make things worse rather than better, just go ahead. Here, I'll leave my gun here for you. If you have no more concern for all of us, especially your own family, just do it. You know, for the first time since I've known you John, I feel let down. I thought you had more fortitude."

Dad turned and walked out. He went a little away from the cabin, and sat down on a cut log. His hands were wet, and there was a pain in his back. He waited.

After what seemed an eternity, John pushed the door open and walked out. He sat down by Dad, handed him his gun, and tears were in his eyes. He said, "Bill, how can I ever thank you? You knew I wouldn't do anything to make things worse for my family. You truly are a friend. No one else would tell me what you just did."

"Well, it was a long shot. I sure had hopes I hadn't misjudged you. Let's just forget this now, and never think of it again. First thing, you better talk to Margaret, and your kids. Tell them what a silly *dope* you are, but that it will never happen again. And John – mean it."

"When you're all settled down, come on over to our cabin for supper. We've got a lot of work to do. I don't know what was the matter with me? I should have seen this some time ago. Now I have to question, how many more people, here in camp, are just about at the end of their rope? We have to give them some direction - some hope, John."

In a small, close camp, there is not much that everyone does not know, and John's crisis traveled like wildfire. When John called for a town meeting the following day, everyone in camp was there.

John walked up front. He was back to his old self, and immediately took charge, "Folks, you all know what happened, and I want to apologize to all of you. There was no call for that, and it will never happen again. Everyone here is short of supplies, but we have all seen long, hard winters

41

before. What did we do then? We have always licked hard times, and we are going to beat this winter too."

There was a wide round of applause for they all knew that the *old steam-engine, John,* was back to his old self.

There was new light in John's eyes, and spunk in his talk. Everyone listened intently as he put forward his logic.

"The first thing to consider is heat. Everyone has wood cut and stacked for winter, and that will probably last; however, when there is time, we will add to those piles. God knows, we've got plenty of wood here."

"The women will be the keepers of the fire. Keep them going, and never let them go out. We will all function much better with heat, and women will be cooking and inside more anyway. These gals never let us down yet, and we know they won't now; besides they need to be inside with the little ones much of the time."

"The next thing is not so easy," said John. "That will be food. I know many of us are already low on it. We will set up groups of men who will keep enough meat hanging in the center of camp to feed everyone here. We have some good hunters."

He went on, "A lot of people in camp are pretty well prepared, but some of us are not, and that is for different reasons. The thing is if we are to all survive, we have to work together, and share what we have. I want three people on this committee that will determine who gets food – what kind, and how much. I want Mary Wilson, Judy Hudson, and myself. We will set that up as soon as this meeting is over. There is to be no questioning of the decisions of this committee. If there are any complaints, they will come directly to me; however, I do not expect any."

"Some of you probably wonder how much food is left in the store. There is some, but very little. That will not be used unless everything else is gone. If it is used, the committee will take it and use it as deemed necessary. A complete list of what is taken will be put in the cash register, and settled when the trucks can get back in."

"Since we have no doctor available, I urge everyone to use caution in all you do. If there is need of medical help, you all know Florence has a good supply, and knows her remedies. She has helped many of us before, and she is not a doctor, but she will do her best for us."

"Everyone will work at keeping the snow shoveled away from our living and work areas. We will do that in shifts.

"For three days a week, we will have learning sessions for children, and we will set that up shortly. Susan Brown will take care of that."

Pedro Martinez handed John a cup of coffee. He took a sip and he continued, "Now, I think that covers the main issues to start with, and we will have weekly meetings, or any necessary emergency meetings."

"There is one other important thing: We are going to be snowbound for some time, so we can't forget an important factor – fun! Yes, that's right, folks. We have to have a little fun. There is no reason in the world to stop the Saturday night dances. On Saturday, we will cook a big pot of soup in the mess hall kitchen. People can put in whatever they want. There will always be plenty of fresh meat, won't there fellows? Deer, rabbits, quail. Someone can throw in a few potatoes, maybe a few carrots, some cooked black beans, some onions - whatever is available."

John talked on, "First, we will eat. Then we will have the meeting, and then if these *fiddler fellers* haven't eaten too much, we'll have a little music - shucks, maybe even a little singing. Are there any questions?"

Matt Hatfield stood up and said, "Heck no, John, not as long as you're in charge. You're the most honest feller I ever knew."

The atmosphere in the camp abruptly changed from hopelessness, to almost excitement about doing something.

"All right, folks, let's get busy. We have a lot of work to do, and we are going to do it together," said John.

Within a few hours, venison was hanging from the big tree in the middle of camp. It was cleaned, skinned, and strung up on a pully rope to let it up and down, and to keep animals away.

Mary Wilson and Judy Hudson were going door-to-door, making inventory lists, and arrangements to set-up the food supply station.

The camp had come to life, and soon blossomed, the most valuable treasure of all – laughter, goodwill, and the spirit of working together for the good of all.

Christmas

Everything in the camp was working well. There were still shortages; however, no one hoarded, no one took advantage of anyone, and we lived on what we had.

It certainly did change our Christmas though. There would be no gifts of any kind that were purchased. Everything given was homemade. For our family, there were no packages from my Grandfather, since the roads were still closed.

There was another big difference. This would be the first Christmas that our family was divided. Sis and many of the other children were not at home. I missed Sis dreadfully. I know she missed us too.

Dad and Mama tried to carry on as usual. Mama was making candy, although it was a very small batch. Dad picked up took his ax and said, "Come on Sis. [Yes, he called both of us girls Sis.] Let's go get that perfect Christmas tree."

We didn't have to walk far to find it, and it was perfect, and the branches were covered with heavy snow. Dad chopped it down, and we pulled it home through the snow. He built a wooden stand, shook the tree off, and stood it up inside. We decorated it with strings of popcorn, and with the special, hollowed-out glass bulbs, that had been passed down from my Grandmother - each bulb with its' own Christmas scene. We carefully put on the icicles, one at a time and every one

straight. Then we finished the tree with candles. After supper, when it was very dark, Dad carefully moved the light from one candle to each of the others, each candle in a metal, clip-on holder. We forgot everything as we watched the magic unfold before our eyes. After a very short time, the candles were all put out, and we ate candy, sang Christmas songs, and thought of Sis, so far away.

On Christmas morning I jumped out of bed and ran to the tree. The weather didn't keep Santa away. There, under the tree, was a present for Dad

– a pair of homemade slippers; a gift for Mama – a nice wooden puzzle; and two gifts for me – a little, rag doll, and a pair of homemade slippers. I loved it. I took the doll, and safely tucked her in bed - my bed. Then with Dad and Mama, we took gifts around to some of the families in camp. There were dolls, slippers, scarves, and hats – all of them Mama made herself.

At every house there was a wonderful feeling. I think it was what you call loving geniality. The camp was no longer just a work camp. We had all become a loving family. It was truly a lovely Christmas.

Deep Into Winter

Even though people were getting along well, and there was no apparent trouble within the camp, hardship and misery had not left us. Many people were ill, and Mama was always busy.

Pedro Martinez was found dead one morning, sitting in his rocking chair before the wood stove. The stove had gone out, but the cabin was still warm. Mama said he probably died from a heart attack. The women washed him, and put his best clothes on, as the men, with pick and ax, chipped away at the frozen, shallow grave. Pedro wore his best white, wedding shirt, and was wrapped in his Navajo blanket. He was buried in a rough, wooden box.

Next Spring, fresh dirt would cover the grave, and it would be covered with rocks. The men made a nice cross with his name on it, and below his name read: "Here Lies a Good Man."

Dad felt bad. He had lost a good friend. After Pedro had been buried for a few days, I looked out our window. I quickly walked over to Dad, took his hand, guided him to the window, and said, "There is a man standing by *Señor* Martinez's grave. What's he doing?"

Dad studied him for a few minutes. "I don't know if I can answer that, Sis. That is Joe White Cloud. He is a Pueblo Indian, probably a friend of Pedro, maybe even a relative."

I asked, "How did he get here?"

"I don't know, but I would guess that he walked. Look at him. He is wearing buckskin pants and jacket, with knee-high moccasins, and they have bear-grease rubbed into them. If you look closely, you can see his snowshoes."

I looked at him, and asked, "Isn't he cold, Dad?"

Dad looked at the Indian, then said, "Maybe, but I doubt it. If he is, he will never show it. Indians are patient, long-suffering, stoical people." Joe White Cloud was standing straight and tall, with an air of peace about him. There was almost a sense of a holy man, standing alone in the white snow in the quiet of the mountains.

"Besides," Dad said, "see how he has the Navajo blanket pulled around him. If he gets cold, he will pull it closer and wrap it up around his head. There is nothing warmer than those blankets, and they will keep you pretty dry too. These Indians have lived in this country a lot longer than we have – hundreds of years before we got here. He will be just fine. You don't have to worry about him."

Mama called, "Are you two going to eat this breakfast before it gets cold? Come on."

Dad, moving toward the table, said to me, "Come on, Sis. Let's eat. You don't have to worry about Joe White Cloud. Believe me, he will be fine. He would not come in the house anyway – even if you asked him. Besides, I'm sure he has jerky and probably other things with him to eat."

The Gift

We had just finished breakfast when there was a knock on the door. John was there.

I looked out the window when Dad was talking to Uncle John. Joe White Cloud was no where in sight.

John came in and sat at the table with Dad and Mama. Mama poured him a cup of coffee.

"You'll never guess what I found hanging from the tree with the venison," he said.

Dad's face brightened. "What did Joe leave there?"

"He left a small bag of dried apricots, and a bigger bag of dried corn," he answered.

"Did he bring it for Pedro?" asked Mama.

"I don't know," answered John. "He always seemed to watch out for him. On the other hand, maybe he knew we needed food and brought it for all of us. All we know is that there were snowshoe tracks by Pedro's cabin. Joe knew Pedro was dead, and he left the food anyway."

"One thing I do know," said Dad, "a young buck will kill you in a second if he thinks you are worthless, on the other hand, Indians are an honorable, good mannered, trustworthy people. Personally, I think the world of them. I think he knew we needed other food than meat."

"Well, let's see what he left," said Mama.

John put a bag on the table. It weighed about ten pounds, and was dried apricots. He said, "There is also a bag of corn in the tree, about twenty-five pounds. If we grind it fine, it will make a good bit of corn bread."

"My, how nice that was," said Mama. "It will help us considerably. Every little bit counts. Bless his heart."

John said, "Bill why don't you come and help me divide this up with everyone. I know it won't be a lot, but it will feed the mind as much as the belly."

The Clutches of Deep Winter

Winter slowly pressed on as we struggled to survive. Spirits were fairly high, although at times people would get discouraged, but most despondency lasted only a short time. We were all working together and the majority of us found joy in our simple work, quiet solitude, and natural beauty.

One morning I got up and looked out of the window - there was no Joe White Cloud; however, we were living in a wonderful, ice palace. All the trees and bushes were delicate lace. It was all snow and ice - a world of white. There was an unbroken quiet and a tranquil peacefulness.

My thoughts were disrupted as Mama called, "Come on, Billy. You can come with me to pass out apples. Sit down and have a bite to eat first, then you bundle up so you stay warm."

The stored apples were rapidly going down, and only one apple was given to each person. The rule was to eat it yourself, eat none of anyone else's, and waste nothing. We had no idea of how long it would be before the supply truck came. The snow was still very deep. Although we had plenty fresh meat, vegetables and fruit were rare, and that part of our life was now missing to a sharp degree.

Mama and I first went to the storage area of the store, picked up the apples, and went cabin to cabin. At every cabin, we were happily greeted. When we were finished, we hurried to our warm cabin to stand with our backs to the wood stove.

After our basic chores were done, the women would often gather at someone's cabin to sew, mend, quilt, and always talk. The men were more inclined to play poker, but also did their share of talking. Wherever people were, the conversation was mainly about the state of our country, or the unrest in Europe. Every week someone was assigned to listen to the radio. Only one news cast a week was permitted, so as to save the radio batteries.

It was Dad's turn to have the poker game. Since Pedro Martinez had died, Jess Carson, had agreed to take his place at the games. He was a former school teacher, turned logger - a quiet, satisfied man.

I took my Christmas doll and went to bed when Mama said. As usual I listened to the men talk. They played a long time, and I went to sleep. After a while I woke up to the raised voices of the men.

Matt Hatfield asked, "Well *fellers* I can't stand all this serious stuff only so long. How about a little nip of good moonshine?"

Of course, they all agreed, and the talk went on.

Dad said, "Jess, you're an educated man. How do you think Roosevelt is doing?"

Being a reserved man, he pretty much repeated what he had heard on the radio the night before. He said, "It seems like the man is on the right track. The CCC boys are doing pretty good I hear. It's employment for those young bucks – a little money to jingle in their pockets. I hear they are employing thousands of them. The government says there are many thousand more that need jobs. They are setting them up everywhere, probably be here soon. It seems they still plan for them to do reforestation and flood control, just like Roosevelt said."

Jess continued, "As far as Social Security, it's a hell - uva deal. Looks like Congress will pass that legislation before long, and people will be getting into it. It sure makes sense to me. People pay into it for their working years, and it will be there when they retire. It's the best security umbrella I've ever seen for us working people."

Jess's teaching training took over and he continued, "Right now there is talk about another new program. They call it the WPA. It's a work program for working men that lose their jobs, and can't find one. The government tells us that there are well over two million people out of work right now. Good men too. There are just no jobs. Roosevelt wants to give these men work. In addition it would give them back their self-respect. That is important to a man. Then there is another thing to worry about. That crazy madman in Europe is out-of-his-mind."

John asked, "Do you mean Hitler?"

"Yeah," replied Jess. "He has withdrawn Germany from the League of Nations. He has ordered entire libraries emptied, and all books burned. He does not want anyone thinking for himself. He also dissolved all the labor unions. Who knows what he is about to do. It seems to me, he is a greedy, power hungry man. I don't like him a bit."

Matt Hatfield interjected, "One good thing did happen. When they finally come to *thar* senses in Washington, and repealed prohibition. That was better than *nothin*."

"Yeah," said John, "that was a blunder anyway. Men are going to drink. There is a limit as to what the government ought to do. Their business is to do the big things we can't do —build roads, bridges, schools, the big stuff. It's our job to take care of our own personal business. There are some things that are not government business. Washington should just keep their noses out of those things."

"Well, your absolutely right there, but I guess we had better work on our own problems here and now," Dad said. "I suppose we better save ourselves before we save the world. Now do you want to play another game, or shall we hit-the-sack?"

"Better call it a night," said John. "I think we better go hunting tomorrow. Meat is getting low."

The Big Cat

The following morning the hunters met at the meat tree in the center of camp. John was there. As soon as Matt arrived, he pointed to the tracks under and around the tree. "Cat," he said.

Matt whistled and said, "It's a big one too. It was tracking wild broncos, and they knew it. Look at the horse tracks."

"The cat stopped here," said John. "It probably knew the fresh meat was here. You can see where it went up the tree."

"Yeah," said Matt. "It circled around a couple of times, and gave that idea up. See over here. It came back to following the wild horses."

"I think we better put the dogs on the trail. If that cat doesn't find food, it will be back."

Matt asked, "Do you think we should call a meeting?"

"No, let's just keep this quiet for right now. We will pass it along to those that need to know. We don't have little kids out much now, so we will just warn the parents. You and the fellows do that while I go get my dogs," said John. "Let's meet back here in an hour, and go out."

The hunters cleared the tracks around the meat tree, and set-out on the hunt. The cat was easy to follow in the snow. Finally they came upon the fresh carcass of an old bronco.

"Seems like they always get the young or the old ones first – easy prey," said Sam Wilson. "At least the cat probably won't be back to camp soon. Let's look around. Maybe we can get it yet today."

"I doubt it," said John. "It has a belly full now, and will be looking for a safe place to sleep. Besides it is getting late. I think we better head back to camp and see if we can't pick up some camp meat on the way back. We can look for the cat again tomorrow. It won't go far until it eats more of this meat."

The next morning the spring rains moved in. It rained for days, and the snow started to recede.

The hunters looked for paw tracks every chance they got, but there were no more signs of the big cat.

John said, "You know these cats can travel thirty-five miles in a day. It may be a long way from here."

The rains were followed by floods, and the small creeks became torrents of rushing water. Mud was everywhere, but welcomed as winter steadily started to wane.

The weather continued to improve, and one day about noon, there was music to our ears. The supply truck lumbered into camp, and the driver was smiling, waving, and honking the horn. What a happy day that was! We had fresh fruit and vegetables, bags of flour, rice, sugar, salt, oatmeal, and everything else we needed.

There was a dance in the camp that night, and we ate very well. We were a happy people. We had survived a severe winter. We had fought hard. We had only lost one man, and that made us sad, but all-in-all, we had won.

Chapter 5

The Hammer Falls

Our joy lasted only for a short period. Shortly after the supply truck arrived, the loggers were notified that the camp was closing. There was no more work. People started leaving immediately. We stayed for a short time as there were still some odd jobs for Dad, and a few other workers. There was some work to take care of closing the railroad, and a couple of the work sites. Dad worked at the camp for awhile, and then he was sent further into the mountains to do work at a site there. It was rumored that it was to be a CCC camp. There were two other families that went with Dad: John and his family, Matt and his wife, and Mama and me.

There was no name for the area we moved to. It was only known by Site Number Three. There were three old shacks there. There was a little stream, with a rickety bridge, with one shack on the south side, along with what was left of a rickety, old barn and two shacks on the north side, where we lived.

I knew Mama didn't much like this set-up, but she made the best of it. At least there was still a pay check. She immediately scrubbed the entire place where we were to live. Dad built bunk-beds. He built one for Sis and me, as she was coming home from school. On the other side of the room, he built another bunk-bed for Mama and himself. It was not so pleasant living here. We had to walk a good mile to get our drinking water, which we

55

got out of a nice, clean, mountain spring.   Needless to say, we were very careful with water. Every time the men had spare time, they helped Matt build a make-shift corral, as he had spotted a number of wild, good-looking broncos. In no time, Matt caught a fine mare and put her in the corral.

One day when we were playing outside, five beautiful horses tore into the area of the corral. They were led by an exquisite, white stallion. The stud reared up and came down upon the fence again and again with his hooves

until an area of the fence was actually broken down. The captured mare escaped, and again ran free with the others.

Matt said, "Well, I declare. I never saw *nothin'* like it. Wow! What I would give to catch that fine, white stud. I just better get with it, and put some serious *think'n* into this."

A few days later, I was playing outside with Little John and her brother. We were picking and eating wild strawberries. We drifted further from camp - further than what was allowed.

Suddenly I stopped dead in my tracks. I said, "Don't move, and what-ever-you do, don't run."

"Why?" asked Little John.

"Look up to the top of that ridge, and tell me what you see."

She grabbed her brother's hand, and asked, "Do you see a mountain lion just stretched out?"

I think it is looking at us I said, "Whatever we do, we can't run! Dad says that is when they think you are something to eat. If we just stay together and walk slow, maybe it won't bother us. We won't run unless we see him run. If it comes after us, then climb the nearest tree, and we'll try to keep him down with my big stick. Ok – let's slowly start moving. Move a little -

stop. Keep doing it, and don't make any noise. Now move. Now stop. Stand still."

Every time we stopped, we looked up at the cat. I felt like my knees were shaking. The cat lifted itself up a little and looked at us; otherwise, it never moved.

"That worked," I said. "Keep doing it."

We kept moving like this until we were very close to the camp, and could no longer see the cat. Then we ran as fast as our legs would carry us, looking behind us all the time. When we reached home, we were all as pale as ghosts, and could hardly catch our breath.

Mama said, "All of you, come inside. Now let's go over this again. You say you saw a mountain lion, laying down, on the rock at the top of the ridge. You started coming home, very slowly. The cat lifted up, so you knew it saw you, but it did not make any moves to come after you. Is that right?"

"Yes, Mama," I answered.

"What in the world were you kids doing that far away from the cabin? You all know that you are to stay close. Why?"

"We didn't mean to go so far, Mama," I answered. "We were just picking strawberries, and I guess we just went too far."

"Think twice before you answer this question. You are not lying to me, are you? This is the truth?"

"Yes, Mama, it is the truth."

"Well, it better be. This is serious, and I don't want to disturb your father, and bring him home for nothing."

"It is the truth, Mama," I answered.

She said, "All of you, sit right here on this bench until I get back. If you move an inch, I will switch you good."

I never saw Mama so upset, so we sat quietly while she went outside and rang the emergency bell. We could hear them talking when Dad got back from the work site.

They had their heads close together, but we could hear a little of what they said, now and then.

"Bill, I think they are telling the truth. You should have seen them when they got back here. They looked like death warmed over. There is no doubt about it, they were scared, but I'm not sure of what they think they saw. Maybe it was a coyote, or a bobcat? I don't know, but I do know, they were scared."

"Well Mama, I never caught her ever telling us lies, and she knows what a lion looks like. I believe her, but I will check on it."

She looked him right in the eye, and said, "If that cat is out there, I don't mind telling you, I am worried. What kind of protection do we have in this hole? My God, I could throw the dishwater outside, through the cracks, and never get the walls wet."

"I know, Honey, but we are not going to be here very long, then we will move into town," Dad said. "I'll take care of it."

My heart sank when I heard Dad say that. I thought to myself, "How can we leave this place? I love it here. I don't want to go to some place that I don't know. I want to stay here."

Dad came inside, and we again told him what had happened. He said, "You three stay inside with Mama." Then looking at John's kids, he said, "I'll tell your mother where you are. All of you stay here."

He said to Mama, "You know where the gun is. I'll be back soon."

Dad took his heavy-duty rifle off the wall, and put extra shells in his pocket. He nodded his head to us and left.

When Dad got back, John and Matt were at our place. "What did *ya'* find?" asked Matt.

"I found new tracks in the soft dirt, just as plain as everything. I found part of a coyote, so the cat had just eaten. That is why it didn't have any interest in the kids. The tracks looks like the ones we found in the winter. It's a big cat."

John asked, "You think it's the same one that has been tracking the broncos?"

"Probably," said Dad. "We know the horses are here, so it's pretty safe to guess the cat does too. Probably the same one, found that the broncos are pretty easy prey, and probably it has been tracking them for some time."

John said, "I'm going to get my hounds. We'll need them. If we are lucky, we can get the cat before dark. We can't let it go this time."

Matt quickly returned, with his gun, ready to hunt. John followed with his gun and the hounds. The dogs were excited. They knew they were going to hunt. One of his dogs always liked me, and he came over and licked my face. "Ugh! He smelled stinky, but he was a nice dog. I liked him.

Soon we could hear the baying of the hounds as the hunters picked up the trail. Soon we heard barking, and we knew they had the cat up a tree. We heard a roar, a yelp, more barking, then a shot, wild yelping, and then quiet. We knew they had their kill.

They gutted the cat, and skinned it in the woods. John took the pelt to make a wall-hanging out of it. I knew it would really be pretty, only it was colored a lot different than our bear - skin rug. The lion was a rich brown and tan. It was a handsome creature, and it didn't look so dangerous anymore, without its' teeth and insides.

The hunters all agreed. The pelt was John's. The men probably would have never gotten it without John's hounds – at least not as fast, or as easy. We all breathed much easier after the big cat was gone; however, the *close to home rule* had a lot more meaning for us than it had before. Mama didn't have to worry so much about us going away from camp anymore. She knew this time we had really learned our lesson.

The Depression Drags On

The following night, both the men and the women played cards. Things were different now, since there were only three men. Mama and Aunt Margaret did some hand sewing, and talked, while the three men played cards with Matt's wife, Rita.

Rita wasn't a drinker. She didn't like it, but she did like her coffee, and she did her share of talking. One thing people liked about her was that she always knew what was going on in the world. They had just started playing, when Rita asked, "What do you boys think of Mrs. Roosevelt?"

Dad said, "She is part of the reason Roosevelt is doing so well. She is the President's ears, so he knows what is going on. I like him more all the time. Most all of his programs are really working for us. You know when you inherit a big mess like he did, and the bottom falls out of everything, it is sure a big job to get things back on track again. He is doing it though. He is a good president, one of the best we have ever had, and he has done the most good for the working man. Eleanor had a lot to do with keeping him informed, and her work helped provide a way for his programs. She has been very responsible."

Rita answered, "You're right, Bill. He is doing a super job. We have really been lucky that we've had work. So many people haven't had any for such a long time. I don't know how they make it. I'm glad things are getting better; however, I just hate the thought that we have no more work here now. It's so sad - just like breaking up a family. I know Matt has some ideas of how to make a good business. He has probably said something to you both about it – the horse ranch?"

"Yeah," said John. "I hear that some people are getting free land. The horses are no problem. All you have to do is catch them and they are yours. You just might have something there, Matt."

Matt looked at John and said, "What are you *goin'* to do, John, when we finish up here?"

"I have already talked to the big *fella* down at the WPA office. When they get organized, they will need a man to do some labor overseeing. That has been pretty much my line of work. I just might go with them. Pay is not what it was here, but at least it is a job. It will put bread on the table, and I've got kids that have to go to school too. You have to think about that."

Rita looked at Dad and said, "Well, Bill, that just leaves you. Do you have any plans?"

Dad answered. "I have already rented a house in Bernalillo. I figure to settle Florence there with the kids. Sis will be going back to school after summer is over, and it won't be long before Little Bill will be starting. I plan to look for work in Bernalillo first."

Rita frowned and answered. "You guys are just so lucky to have these youngsters. I wish we had been that lucky."

Dad patted Rita on the hand and said, "Yeah, we sure have been lucky - good kids, and healthy too. I've got to feed them though. If I don't find work around here, think I'm going to hop a passing freight and check out work in Arizona and California. I hope to pick up something with the railroad. When times were so bad last winter, and after the roads cleared, Dad sent us some money to help us get through. With that and the little we have managed to save, we have a little bit put aside to help us make some changes. Meanwhile, I'm putting the word out that I'm looking for work."

Rita started to cry and mumbled, "I just hate to think of us all going in different directions. It is breaking up a family – our family, even though we aren't blood. We've never been closer to anyone than you guys!"

Mama always knew the power of food. She said, "I've got a pot of coffee, and made a fresh pie today. The girls picked us some fresh berries. I guess we better try that pie so we don't hurt their feelings."

The Barn

We had no more trouble with animals the rest of the summer. After the cat problem had been taken care of, we did stay close to the buildings. We liked one building so well that we started playing there a lot - the old barn.

Apparently someone had used the barn to cut a lot of lumber. There was a big pile of sawdust right in front of the big front doors. We started climbing up the ladder, made our way to the front loft opening, and jumped into the big pile of sawdust. We did this time and again. We had loads of fun.

One time when it was my turn to jump, I did. When I hit the sawdust pile, I bent over and tried to catch my breath. I couldn't speak. I slouched down into a seated position, and pulled my foot toward me. There was blood, and lots of it. There was also a nail that had run completely through my foot.

Sis had seen everything. She ran toward me, and said, "Just be still. Everything will be OK. I'm going to get Mama." And she was gone.

Mama didn't look very well when she reached us. Her color was not good, but she talked to me in a calm way. She said, "We're going back to the cabin. You will be just fine, so just try to relax."

She looked at Sis, and said, "I'm going to pick her up and carry her to the cabin. You just walk along beside me and hold her foot up. Try to stay even with me, and don't move it any more than you have to."

When we got back, she sat me on the front steps and looked at my foot. Then she went into the house and collected things she needed, and cleaned her hands thoroughly.

When she came back, she sent Sis into the house to watch the water heating. When it was hot, Sis brought the bucket outside. When the temperature was right, Mama poured the amount of water that was needed into the sterile bucket that she had just cleaned. She added the correct amount of disinfectant. She put my foot into the bucket, and said, "Honey,

we are going to soak your foot for a while. Then I'm going to give you something to swallow, and it won't taste good, but take it all."

While my foot was soaking, Mama washed and disinfected Dad's pliers. When she saw my eyes getting heavy, she felt around my foot, lifted it up a little, and pulled out the nail.

The pain was overwhelming, and as soon as I could talk, I said, "Oh, Mama, it hurts!"

"I know, Honey. It will get better soon though. Just hang in there," she said.

The blood was just squirting out and she encouraged it to do so. She explained to Sis, "Since this is a puncture wound, it is better to let it bleed for some time. It will help clean it out. Since this happened in a barnyard, it is essential that it is well cleaned, and kept very clean."

When Mama was satisfied it had bled enough, she switched buckets again and I had to sit with my foot in clean, sterilized water. After a time she checked for bleeding, wrapped my foot in sterile bandages, and propped it up on a pillow. Twice a day, this became a routine - clean the wound, soak in disinfectant, bandage, keep raised, and most important of all, watch for infection. Everything seemed to be going well.

From the day I jumped on the nail, every time Dad came home, he would look at my foot, and talk with Mama about it.

Dad spent more time reading to me and Sis. One day he said to me, "Well, Sis, I don't think we will be going fishing for the rest of this summer. We'll have to wait for that foot to heal, but we will go again. Just do everything your Mama tells you."

When they were alone, he asked Mama, "Do you think we need to get her down to Bernalillo to see a doctor? Do you think there is a chance of her getting lockjaw? What about gangrene?"

"I don't know what to tell you, Bill. I don't see any sign of infection. Certainly there is a real chance of lockjaw and also gangrene; however, I don't see any sign of either. We did bleed it. Actually the wound looks very good considering. Whether or not she might get gangrene or lockjaw, I honestly can't tell you. It might be worse taking her to a hospital where there are all kinds of germs. Not only that, I'm sure the trip would tire her out.   Bill, it is eighty miles to the nearest doctor, so that is 160 miles round trip, and it is hot enough here, but much hotter in town. This summer has been very stressful on her anyway, and God only knows how many diseases are rampart in the city. Not only that - what can the doctor do that we have not already done? He would just tell us to go home and keep it clean. She is young, strong, and healthy, so I personally feel that we should just keep doing what we have been doing. If you are asking me if it can kill her, yes, it most certainly can, but we have done our best under the circumstances, so I think we would do better to just let nature take its' course. At this point, I really can't see exposing her to anything else. That could be worse."

"I see your point, and I trust your judgment, Honey," he said.

Chapter 6

The Big Transition

Summer was just about over. We packed everything we owned and moved to Bernalillo. It was the biggest change in my life ever. Things were new to me, and we had moved away from all of our friends, and all that had meaning to me.

As soon as we got into a house, Mama cleaned everything. As we were getting settled, Dad was looking for work. He looked for work locally first, but found absolutely nothing. He knew money was scarce and would not last long, so he jumped a freight train, and went to Arizona, and on to California, looking for work.

We were on our own. Mama took in washing and did big tubs of ironing - mainly men's white shirts.

It was not long before Dad came back. Jobs were as scarce as hen's teeth in the western states as they were in New Mexico.

One day I heard Dad and Mama talking. Dad said, "Honey, I think you better stay here with the girls until I find a job."

"What are you going to do, Bill?" Mama asked.

"If I don't find any work, I think I'll do the same as John did, and go to work for the WPA. Like John said, 'It puts bread on the table.'"

Within a very short time Dad did go to work. It was work on the roads and bridges. There was a lot of travel involved.

Mama did not like the idea of Dad being away from home, but she was grateful that he had a job with a regular pay check. When Dad told her she said, "Thank God, and thank President Roosevelt. He is a life saver to us."

In some ways life was better for us living in town. We had running water. We had a real bath room - inside the house. We had electric lights, and we could listen to the radio any time we wanted to, that is, if Mama let us. However, we all felt like something was missing in our lives. We didn't like our lack of freedom, not seeing our friends, but most of all, we missed not seeing Dad. We really missed his reading to us every night.

The plan was that Dad would be working where the job took him. Mama, Sis, and I would live in the rented house in town, until such time as we could be together again. We didn't like this situation, but that was what we had to do.

Dad was gone a lot. Construction took him all over the state. He did not mind the work, but he didn't like it as well as he had liked working on the railroad, and he hated being away from us.

When summer came, and Sis was out of school, we locked up the house, and followed Dad. We took our clothes, our bedrolls, and our gas camp stove. We took some personal items, and essential cleaning supplies. We tried to take only absolute essentials. We moved a lot, sometimes once every two or three weeks, sometimes our stay was longer. Everything depended on how much time Dad's work took.

Much of the time, we lived in small - 12' by 12' - roadside cabins. They were always dirty, and Mama spent most of her time cleaning, cooking, and doing laundry. However, we were happy. We were together again.

First Trip In To Old Mexico

The first summer we went with Dad, we went to the most far southwestern part of New Mexico. This was the first extended time all of us were on the road. We followed the Rio Grande River south until we got to Las Cruces. This was a different kind of country. The Rio Grande was much bigger, and ran a muddy brown. The trees were scrub willows, and grew mainly along the river edge. The mountains were much more rugged.

Las Cruces was different than Bernalillo. It was just a little north of the boarder crossing, where there was a constant exchange of Mexicans and Americans crossing the bridge. When we crossed the Mexican border, it was not so very different for us. We probably heard as much Spanish spoken at home as we did in this foreign country. It seemed strange to me to stop at the border and have our car checked.

The guard approached our car, reached out his hand for Dad's papers. He smiled at me and said, "Buenos dias, Señorita."

"Buenos dias," I answered.

He smiled and waved us on. Dad drove into Juarez - Old Mexico. He parked the car, and we went shopping.

Dad said, "Don't eat or drink anything while we are here. When you are in any unknown area, it is better to err on the safe side - especially with food and water. However, if you find a nice pair of shoes, you can have them."

Mama, Sis, and I bought soft, leather, woven shoes. Mama told us that these shoes were called *huaraches* - that is the Mexican word for the kind of shoes we bought. They were hand made, and they were a low heel sandal. They were the most comfortable shoes in the world, and we all loved them.

The first thing we learned about them was to soak them in water, and wear them wet the first time. After that, they were perfect, and they lasted forever.

After we paid for our shoes, we crossed the bridge again. A guard asked what we had purchased, and Dad told him. He looked our packages over, and told us to have a good day, and waved us on. When we were back in the United States, we continued on our way west. As we left Deming, we saw fields of chili, and groves of pecan trees. Dad said we were now only about thirty miles north of Old Mexico, and we were traveling almost parallel with the border.

It was not long before we crossed the Continental Divide. Dad explained to us that the Divide was a ridge going along the Rocky Mountains, and it divided which way the water ran - side west, going to the Pacific Ocean, and the side east going to the opposite direction - toward the Atlantic Ocean by way of the Gulf of Mexico. He also told us that the Divide affected the weather of our country.

Not long after we crossed the Divide, we entered Lordsburg. Now we were only about twenty miles, or so, from the Arizona border. Lordsburg was an interesting place, but we moved on into Arizona, to see the open pit copper mines, on our way to Uncle John's house. That was just something Dad wanted us to see. When we got to the mine, Dad drove along the edge, and we stopped. As I looked down into the gigantic, hollowed, crater, I was amazed to see a full size train. It circled all the way to the bottom, where it was loaded, and sent back to the top. I had never seen anything like that before.

We would have liked to have spent more time in these areas, but Dad had to get back for work, so we had to move right along. Dad would be working in the same area as his old friend, John, and arrangements had been made for us to stay with him, and his family, for a short time during the summer.

John was now living in Silver City, between the Gila National Forest and the Mogollon Mountains. This was the area of the Gila Cliff Dwellings, and also the area that was famous for the old, Indian Pottery. Silver City was sitting on the Continental Divide - just a hair to the west. This area was very much like the area we lived in at the Jemez Mountains. I felt quite at home here, and I liked it.

When we arrived at Uncle John's house, it was like a family reunion. Everyone was so glad to see each other. I thought Little John was going to break all of my bones, she hugged me so hard.

Uncle John said, "You two girls go out to the rabbit pens, and pick out a nice rabbit. We will have it for dinner."

I don't know quite what I thought about that. It was one thing to eat venison, but killing dinner and then eating it immediately was another; however, I would never let Little John know what I was feeling. I sure didn't want her to know how squeamish I was so I just followed her along.

She said, "Have you ever killed a rabbit before?"

"No," I answered. "What do you want me to do?"

She asked, "Has Uncle Bill ever told you what the Indians do before they kill meat that they eat?"

"No, Dad never told me that. What do they do?"

"You know that the American Indians are a very respectful, not only toward people, but also to animals. When they are about to kill an animal, they talk to it first. They tell it how beautiful it is, and how much they respect it. Then they thank the animal for sacrificing itself that the people may live. Then they quickly kill it, eat it, and never waste any of it. It is all used for the good of the people."

"Oh, that is sad, but actually very beautiful," I said.

Little John picked up a handsome brown rabbit, with shades of tan and white running through its fur. She gently patted it, talked to it in a soothing voice, and slit its throat. The animal gave a quick jerk, and died. She showed me how to bleed it, remove the fur, and then gut it. She took the fur and carefully spread it out to take care of later. We cut the rabbit up. We took it into the house and cooled it in ice cold, vinegar water.

We had a wonderful supper that night, although I must admit that I really did not enjoy the rabbit very much, although in time I learned to like it. It did touch something deep inside of me though. I don't think I ever ate another piece of meat that I was not grateful to that animal for giving its life that I might live.

After supper, there was constant talking. There was so much to catch up on.

The first thing Dad asked Uncle John was what had happened to Matt Hatfield and his wife, Rita.

John laughed, and said, "Well, Matt got his government land, and caught his wild horses. He got his ranch started. I hear he is doing very well. He did give up his side business though. I guess it got a little too hot in the bootleg business. That was smart of him though. It was just a good thing he was never caught. If he had been, instead of running a respectable ranch, he would probably be warming a seat in jail. Really, I could never understand his thinking on that subject anyway, but it is good he did get out of it. "

Dad said, "I'm really glad things worked out for him and Rita. They were both good workers, and we've all had some hard times in this country. I'm happy for them. And how have things been for you?"

"I can't complain," answered John. "The WPA work is not what I would have chosen, but it has been a fairly good living. We are doing jobs that this country needs done, and the pay is dependable. We have done a lot of bridge and road work – same stuff you've been doing. We have also done some schools. They are good schools, and the benefits of that will last for years to come. I guess it is a good exchange. At least, Roosevelt's programs are getting the country back on its feet. There have been ups and downs, but it is working."

Dad answered, "It's been a long time since I lost my job, and I haven't even had a nibble on a railroad job. I hear on the radio that unemployment is still high, even with the WPA and the CCC camps now operating. Last paper I saw said something like over eleven million men are still unemployed. How could that many people have survived without jobs for as long as this crisis has lasted? I don't know what we would have done without the work that President Roosevelt started. I think we have to give him credit."

John said, "A lot of people would have died without these work programs. I don't know what to expect now as far as work is concerned. It seems to me that things are certainly getting better here, but I can't help but wonder what the *mad Austrian* is doing. He could change things in this country mighty fast. He talks peace, but I don't think anyone buys that. Hell, he started compulsory military draft again. What does that tell you?"

Dad answered, "I don't know. Well Roosevelt has been a dandy president! He sure did have a big mess dumped into his lap, and he has done very well getting our country moving again. I suppose if Hitler is as crazy as we all think, he sure could make trouble for us all."

Summer is Gone

Summer slipped away like wildfire. The national elections were coming up soon, and work continued to slowly grow. There was fun in our lives again.

Little John and I spent day after day playing in the mountains and all around town. I got to know some of the other kids. We played games, and hiked. We had never ending baseball games. We couldn't wait for supper and dishes to be done so we could play ball again. We ate well. We had a nice, clean place to live. We even went to Saturday night dances again. We had friends to visit with, people who knew and loved us, people who had gone through the same hard times that we had gone through.

It was a good time, but all too soon it was over. It was fall - time to go back to Bernalillo. It was also time for Sis to go back to school. We hugged, kissed, and said our good-byes to Uncle John and his family. Dad drove us back to Bernalillo, and he returned to work any place his work took him.

Not long after Sis had started school again, and Mama had cleaned, and everything was back in order, I received a package from my Dad. It was a beautiful book, written by Willa Cather. It was called <u>Death Comes For The Archbishop.</u> I was thrilled. It was the first book of my very own. There was a note in it from Dad. It said:

Dear Billy,

I know your reading is not real good yet, but I know you can read this. If you have any trouble with words, write them down and have your mother or Sis, help you with them. When I get home, I expect you to read it to me.

Love, Dad

Mama told me that the book was about a young, Catholic Bishop that was sent to the Southwest as a missionary. His name was Bishop Jean Marie Latour. He was accompanied by his boyhood friend, Father Joseph Vaillant. She said it was very wild when they came to our part of the country, and villages and pueblos were far apart, and sometimes the people were very hostile to strangers. The priests settled in Santa Fe, and Father Latour built an amazing church there. She said the priests traveled from one Indian settlement to another, and learned the ways of the Indians, and their customs. She said they traveled sort of like we were doing right now, except travel was much harder. They usually traveled on horseback, followed by pack-mules.

Mama picked up my book and looked at it. She said, "Just take your time, and if you get stuck, call me, and I will help you. You can ask Sis too, but if she is doing home work, call me instead."

I started reading my book immediately. My reading was slow. In the beginning, I had a lot of words going into my notebook to study, but gradually the reading became easier. It was a wonderful story, and once I started reading, I could not seem to put my book down.

One night when Sis was working on her homework and Mama was in the kitchen, I was stretched out on the bear rug reading my book, when I felt like someone was looking at me. I looked up at the window, and there was a man standing outside the window watching us. I put my book down, pretended I didn't see the man, stretched, and walked into the kitchen.

I quietly said to Mama, "There is a man standing outside the window, looking at us."

"Do you know him?" asked Mama.

"No," I answered.

Mama and I walked back into the living room. We saw no one outside. Mama went outside and looked around. No one was there.

Mama said, "Don't say anything to anyone about this. If you see him again, say something like you are tired and think you are going to bed. Then get up, and walk into your room."

Every night I read, I watched for the man. This went on for some time, and then one night, he was there again.

75

I stretched, rolled my eyes toward the window, and said, "Mama, I'm hungry. Can I have something to eat?"

She knew what I was telling her right away. She asked Sis if she wanted something to eat. She just shook her head, and continued her home work.

When we got to the kitchen, Mama asked, "Did you see him again?"

I shook my head, "Yes." She handed me a cookie, and told me to go back to the living room, and keep reading my book.

Warrior Mother

Mother picked up her old, wooden rolling pin. She quietly slipped out the back door, and walked to the front window. The man was so busy watching Sis and I that he did not even seem to be aware that Mama was there.

Suddenly she attacked. She screamed at him, and hit him again and again. As soon as he realized what was happening, he tried to push her away, but she just kept hitting him. Finally he got away from her and ran like everything down the street.

Mrs. Martinez, our next door neighbor, heard the commotion and came running outside. She was one of the few neighbors that had a telephone and she called the police.

When the police arrived, they checked the house and all around it for footprints. It was hard to see since it was dark, but they did find some footprints in the soft dirt.

The policeman asked if Mama wanted to file a complaint. She said she had not thought about it. She told him she had no idea who the man was, but we knew it was not the first time he had been looking into our house.

The policeman told her it would be a good idea to file a report on it, and said that they would keep an eye on our house.

Mama thanked the police and invited Mrs. Martinez in for a cup of coffee. She did have coffee with Mama and they eventually became good friends. Every time Mrs. Martinez made hot chili, she brought a big bowl to Mama because she knew she liked it. It was so hot that Sis and I could not even eat it.

The police never found out who the man was, although they did find blood in our front yard. Mrs. Martinez laughed, and said he probably would never go to the police.

She said, "What is he going to say? Maybe: 'That little tiny woman beat me up'. No, he won't do that. Besides, the police would just ask him what he had been doing looking into our window, and he had been seen twice. No, don't worry, he was up to no good, but he won't want to talk to the police. Forget him."

Shortly after this happened, Dad came home. He said he would be home for a few days. There was a hold - up with needed supplies, so he was off for a short time.

Chapter 7

Pueblo de Taos

The second day Dad was home he asked, "How would you kids like to go on a little trip? We don't often have the opportunity to travel for pleasure, so I think it would be a good idea. What do you think about that?"

"Sure," we both answered. "Where are we going?"

"Well, I thought you might like to go to Taos and also to the Taos Pueblo. You have been to Indian Pueblos and villages before, but I think you will find this a lot different. We can leave early in the morning, and it will be a very long day."

We were all excited. Mama liked it because she thought it would get our minds off the man looking in our window. Dad just liked the idea of us all going somewhere together as a family. Sis and I just liked to go anywhere.

The next morning Dad and Mama were ready. Dad had taken care of the car. He filled the gas tank, and checked every thing. The car was ready to go.

Mama had filled the water bag with drinking water and hung it on the front bumper. Then she made lunch to take with us. She made peanut butter and jelly sandwiches, hard-boiled eggs, cut-up carrots, and took a bag of oatmeal cookies.

Early in the morning, we all ate breakfast - oatmeal with milk and brown sugar, toast, and a small glass of orange juice. We piled into the car and left in the dark. Knowing the area, Sis and I soon grew bored and tired, and we both were lulled to sleep with the motion of the car moving quietly along the highway. As we drifted off, we could hear Dad and Mama talking about Taos, and when they got married. They laughed.

When we woke up we were nearing a high hill. Dad, seeing that we were awake explained things as he pointed them out.

He said, "Look straight ahead of us. That high butte right in front of us is called La Bajada Hill. It was built by volcanic eruptions that occurred in the Jemez Mountains thousands of years ago. Now when the sun hits the rock, it glistens and shimmers in the light like fine jewelry. The hill is a fair climb. Actually between Albuquerque and Santa Fe, the altitude increases by about a thousand feet."

Just before we drove up La Bajada Hill, we saw the turn - off to the Santa Domingo Indian Pueblo going to the west. "That is where Joe White Cloud lives, or at least he did," Dad said. "His house is close to the Rio Grande River, and the people there grow a lot of what they eat. It is easy to irrigate, and things grow well. The soil is very rich. That area is a lot different than what you will see in Taos today."

It seemed like a very short time and we were in Santa Fe. Dad got off the main highway and drove into the heart of town. At the Plaza, he showed us the Palace of the Governor. He said, "That is where Governor Lew Wallace wrote <u>Ben Hur.</u> He actually lived in the building then. It is an interesting structure. It was the seat for a number of governments - first for Spain, then for Old Mexico. For a short time, actually during the Civil War, it was taken over by the Confederate Forces, and finally it became the seat of government for the United States and eventually New Mexico. There are hundreds of years of interesting history in that old building."

The Palace of the Governors at Santa Fe, NM

As Dad turned off the Plaza, he pointed out the church that Father Lamy built in the 1800s. It is called Saint Francis Cathedral. Dad said, "The Cathedral is an unpretentious building, but of unsurpassed quality. It took Father Lamy a long time to find the proper stones for building his dream church. He found the stone about fifteen miles from Santa Fe. It is an unusual golden color, and when the sun hits it just right, it looks like refined gold. When you walk inside the church, the first thing that catches your attention, are the beautiful leaded windows. They are a superb work of art. The entire church is a rose in a garden of thorns."

Mama said, "That church gives you a feeling of being with God. I can't explain it, but a wonderful feeling floods your whole being when you walk inside. It is a calm, serene, accommodating place."

A short distance away Dad pointed out The Loretto Chapel.

Mama said, "The nuns call it, The Chapel of our Lady of the Light."

Dad said, "There is an interesting story about it. The Chapel was built for the nuns after the Cathedral was built. There had not been nuns there before. It took five years to build the little chapel, and just before it was finished, the man building it died, but the staircase to the choir loft had not been built yet. That loft was tucked away in the back, and there was no way to get to it except by way of a high ladder. The choir loft was seldom used because the nuns were afraid to climb the steep ladder. Builders and the very best carpenters were called in, but no one knew how to build such a challenging staircase."

"The story goes that one day an old, grey-haired man came on a donkey and offered to build the staircase. Being at their wits end, the Church agreed. When it was finished, the old man and his donkey quietly disappeared without pay, and the staircase was exquisite. It was art in its' purest form. No one knew who he was, or where he came from. Never any trace of him was found. Some people believed he was St. Joseph. Others laughed at that, but who knows? The story has persisted."

"Dad," I asked, "do you think it really was St. Joseph?"

"Honey, I don't know. Who am I to say?"

Mama said, "There are a lot of things that people just do not understand. Sometimes a child lives when by all human standards should die. Sometimes a person is seriously injured, and no one thinks it is possible to recover, but that person fully recovers and lives a normal life. How can we know about this marvelous staircase? Maybe it was St Joseph. Maybe it was the 'Carpenter' himself. Everyone who ever sees the staircase says it is a miracle. It is strong, durable, and perfect in every way. Sometimes we simply have to believe that some of the things we see truly are miracles. I think I could believe that. I believe God gives us miracles occasionally to give us hope. As far as people thinking the building of the staircase is a miracle is fine with me. It makes me feel good to think that."

Dad checked his pocket watch and said, "If we are going to get to Taos today, we better be moving along. We will come back again to Santa Fe and spend a lot more time here. I love this town, and I never get tired of coming here. You know your mother and I lived here once."

Dad moved back to the main highway and we headed north again. The area was changing and the altitude became higher. Soon we passed Tesuque Pueblo, and then we drove through the Santa Clara Pueblo. We could see the much talked about flat mountain, Black Mesa, across the Rio Grande. It is considered sacred by the Indians and other peoples are not allowed to go there. During the Pueblo Indian Revolt, the Spanish soldiers tried to capture the Indians that had gone to Black Mesa for safety, but the Spanish soldiers never were able to capture them, nor even get to the top of the mesa.

Shortly after passing Espanola, we entered the Rio Grande River Gorge. The highway ran close to the fast, turbulent river as the outpouring of water plunged over the big, exposed rocks. Dad knew the area very well and soon pulled across the road and drove down a donkey path that led to a beautiful spot on the edge of the river. It was a small, grassy area, with a few big, cotton-wood trees, and there was a foot bridge crossing the river. As we got out of the car, you could hear the fast water and look up and see the deep, blue sky high above the lip of the ravine, and it was an awe - inspiring feeling. Mama spread the blanket on the grass and we had a lovely lunch. Then we were on our way again, winding up into the higher mountains.

Dad was right about Pueblo de Taos. It was a place different. The people seemed to be pretty much the same, but the buildings were awesome, very impressive. As we sat in the car while Dad talked with the Indian meeting us, I looked the place over.

The buildings seemed like a never ending apartment house, going on and on. They seemed to grow out-of-the ground. They was built of heavy logs, thinner poles, with mud and straw bricks, and the entire project was covered with a mud plaster. Dad told us that the pueblo probably had a thousand or more rooms. The main floor was level with the ground, with the higher levels each set-back. They were terraced. The entire village was

from one to four stories high. There were no windows or doors on the first level. Entry was from the ground level roof, and ladders went up to the top level, or down into the ground.

Outside were the usual ovens for baking bread. They were the same as the other villages that I had seen. Like the others, there was red chili hanging along entrances, drying in the warm southwestern sun.

There were happy, free people all around. Two young bucks came running past us. They were dressed in leather, wearing feathers, and bells. There were women and they appeared to be dancing. They moved to the beat of the drum that was playing. The dancers were clean, with their black hair pulled back from their faces, and braided down their backs. They were dressed in black skirts that just came above their soft, flexible leather moccasins. Their blouses were blues, purples, or red velvet, and their jewelry was silver and turquoise worn on both arms and around their neck, and waists.

Dad came back and said, "Those boys you just saw and the women are dressed in their ceremonial clothes. You can hop out of the car if you want to, and we will walk around the Pueblo."

Walking around was so exciting. The smell was like a whiff of heaven. There was bread baking in the outside ovens. There were pots of green chili cooking and fresh tortillas. There were burros, goats, and sheep wandering around, kids playing games, and people in Indian dress everywhere. It was so fun. We all loved it, and time to go home came too soon.

Just before we climbed into the car, we stopped and looked at a sand painting. It was so beautiful, and when I asked Dad about it he said, "That is an Indian prayer. It is made of colored sands, and when it is all finished, it is blown away by the winds."

The way home flew by. Our heads were full of the wonderful things we had seen during the day. We talked and talked on the way home, and stopped in Santa Fe at a little grocery store. Mama bought store bread, lunch meat, a small jar of mayonnaise, a jar of dill pickles, and pop, which was a real treat for us. Dad found a nice place to eat, and after eating, it was a non-stop drive home. We napped for a while, but shortly Dad called us.

"Wake up you sleepy heads if you don't want to miss this beautiful night." It was like daylight. The moon was full, and it was as bright as day. You could see everything and there wasn't a car on the road. We rolled down the car windows, and gazed at the moon and the hills bathed in moonlight. The cool air bathed our faces, and the smell of sage and juniper filled the air. Now I didn't feel one bit tired. All I could think of was the wonderful things we had just seen. There was a peaceful quiet in the car, as we all gazed at the bright night sky. It was the end of a perfect day.

School Trip

Sis was doing very well in school. She got along with everyone, and made good grades. When her class was going on a field trip, Sister asked Mama if she would be a chaperon.

Mama said, "I would love to go along; however, I have no one to leave Billy with. If I can take her, I'll be glad to go."

"No problem," answered Sister. "Just bring a lunch for each one of you. We will supply drinks, and plan for an all-day trip."

We met at the school, and retraced our route – same one our family usually took up to the Jemez Mountains when we came from Bernalillo or Albuquerque. The old Indian Pueblo ruins, we were visiting today, were just a short distance away – just off the main highway.

We dressed to do a lot of walking, and took a sweater along just in case of a weather change. We also took scarves to cover our mouths in case of a sand storm. In the Southwest the sandstorms can be fierce, and they often come up quite fast. They can darken the sky for miles and miles.

The ruins, that we were to visit, were left from an old time Indian settlement, very early Indians. They were believed to be a peaceful people. We had always been told that a lot of the Indians in our area were originally cliff-dwellers. There were many areas like the one we were visiting, but numbers of them had been abandoned years before, and simply disintegrated. No one seemed to know why the Indians left. People who studied this had thought that possibly the Navajo, Apache, or the Comanche, being more of a war-like people, had driven the original dwellers out. Others thought that possibly the weather, and lack of water was the reason. The same pattern of Indians building, moving, and then leaving, happened in Arizona, and up into Colorado, and further into Utah.

As we approached the ruins, I remembered them. My family had been here before, when Dad was with us. There was an outside wall, it was probably three or four foot thick adobe. Much of it was in disarray.

Adobe is a brick, made of mud and straw, and sun-dried. At the ruins, what was left of the wall wrapped a large, round, sunken adobe building. Dad had told us the building was called a kiva. It was one room, with a fire pit in the center. There were shelves along the outside, and hooks to hang things on. The floor was swept clean, and the walls had the look of whitewash. There were no doors, nor windows. The only opening was through the ceiling, and there was a ladder for entrance and exit. The Kiva was used for religious, and other important community meetings. Much of what Sister told us, Dad had read to us many times before.

As soon as we had all arrived, Sister started talking to our group. She said:

"These ruins were probably built by the Pueblo Indians. They were often attacked by the Navajo, and Apaches. These walls are so thick because the Indians used the walls for protection, and they were easy to make, and all the material was here. The thick walls in the fences and buildings served a number of purposes - as I said before, protection was an important thing, plus arrows probably would not go through them. In addition the thick walls kept the buildings cool in the summer, and warm in the winter. It was a very practical way to build, and a very smart way."

A student asked, "Sister, why are the walls fallings down?"

She answered, "These walls are very, very, old. White men did not come into this area until around the 1600s, and we actually do not know how much earlier the Indians were here. If you want to do a research paper, you could visit the old adobe church in Santa Fe. It has walls about four feet thick. It was built in the early 1600s and it is still in use. Thank you, Edgar, for that question, and if you do want to do a paper, we will talk about it at school."

Sister continued, "These Indians that lived here probably sat on animal skins, and ate hot, rolled tortillas. They were a peaceful people. They farmed - grew corn, squash, and seemed to love fruit. The Rio Grande River valley has rich, fertile land, and grows many things if irrigated. I think chili has always been a good crop for people of this area. It tastes good, grows well here, and is very healthy."

It was lunch time, and we climbed up the ladder and went outside. I was surprised how far we could see while we were standing on top of the Kiva. The sky was a deep blue, and the white clouds seemed to be big, fluffy pictures. It was so pretty. It was nice, and warm. As I looked at the old ruins, my mind could picture the parade of brown skinned people walking the same areas we were all standing on at this moment. I could not help thinking of all the people who had been in this land so long before we were here. What wonderful foresight they had, and how much they had accomplished, and with so little. They were a good, simple people, and they must have been a very intelligent people.

My mind went back to Joe White Cloud - the Indian that contributed to our living in time of our urgent need. I felt I understood him much better now, and I didn't fear him anymore. I even knew where he lives now. If he were here today, I would say, "I'm proud to know you, Joe White Cloud." I think he might have even smiled - well, maybe just a little.

The rest of the day passed quickly. There was a short period of questions and answers, and then we were on our way home again. It had been a great day, and we thanked Sister for asking us.

She smiled and said, "It was a pleasure having you, and thank you for your help. I hope we can do it again."

Chapter 8

Back on the Road

The school year had finished, and again we were packing – taking only what we absolutely needed. Mama would carefully pack the things we valued, but did not want to take on the road for fear we would lose them, and of course, the problem of space. She wrapped each of our Christmas ornaments that my grandmother had brought over from England so many years before. We tucked as many precious items away in the big trunk as possible. I would leave my new book, and I hated that as my reading was getting easier every day, and I enjoyed reading.

Slowly the things dear to us were safely packed away - pictures, a special dress, my only extra pair of shoes, any items of personal value, near and dear to our hearts.

Dad would be in Bernalillo to pick us up at the end of the week, and we would spend the summer traveling with him again. He said we would be going to Roswell, where he was working.

When Dad arrived, we were ready to go. We were all so glad to see each other. We had missed so many things because of being apart. We really missed Dad when he was gone.

We had supper together that night and it was wonderful to be sharing a meal together again. I never realized what an important aspect such as talking had been in our lives. That night we talked and talked. Of course, we had to tell Dad everything that had happened since he had left.

The following morning, we closed the house up, locked the doors, and left bright and early. We had talked when Dad got home last night about the new book he had given me. He was surprised how far I had read. As we were traveling, and as soon as we were settled down riding, the book came up in our conversation.

I asked Dad, "Are we going to Acoma like Father Latour and his guide, Jacinto did? Are we going to see the pueblo and old church?"

"No," Dad said. "That will be out of our way, and we don't have time to see that today, but we can see something else from your book."

"Darn!" I said. "I wanted to go there. Is it true that the Indians threw the priest over the cliff? Wasn't that a mean thing to do, Dad?"

"Maybe we can go some other time," Dad said. "We just don't have time today. As far as that being mean, I would not say that it was mean. You see the Indians have their own laws, and the way they looked at it was that it was the priest who broke the law. If you remember, the priest accidentally killed the young Indian and he understood the Indian law. The priest knew he had done a bad thing, and he accepted his punishment. The story goes that the priest made no protest when the Indians took him. As far as that being true, I don't know, but I do think that is possible."

"If we don't see Acoma, what are we going to see today?" I asked.

We will be going through Albuquerque and we can stop and see the Old Town Plaza, if you would like. "Do you remember what that was in your book?"

"I think so. Wasn't that an important place that Bishop Latour and his friend and helper, Father Vaillant had visited many times?"

"Yes," answered Dad. "Remember the Bishop made many missionary trips. It was his job to marry people, take care of baptisms, say mass, and take care of all church business. Now Santa Fe was the main headquarters for the church; and that was officially where Father Lamy actually lived; however, Albuquerque was the next most important place."

"Dad, why do you call Bishop Latour Father Lamy?" I asked.

"Well Sis," he said, "you've got me there. That is what people usually call him around here, but I guess I don't know. You see he was a Frenchman, and possibly Lamy is some version of that name, but I don't know for sure. I guess you and I have some research to do. Don't we?"

"Yes, I guess we do," I answered.

Albuquerque

It was a short drive from Bernalillo south to Albuquerque. We drove by Sis's old school, where she first went away to school, when we lived in the mountains. It was nice to see Sis's old school. After we passed the school, we wound slowly down to the bed of the Rio Grande River, and to "Old Town." The sky was a deep, dark, blue with big fluffy clouds, and the weather was warm and fabulous.

Dad parked just off the plaza, and we got out of the car and walked. The plaza itself was very nice. There were shade trees, and benches to rest on. In the center there was a raised gazebo - an old Spanish, open, garden platform on which a *mariachi* band was playing. The band, and their Mexican music, was so beautiful and so lively that it made your feet want to dance. There were three musicians, and they all had big, fancy hats on, which Dad called *sombreros*. They were all dressed in solid black pants, black wedding shirts, and black belts with big, sterling silver buckles, and black, shiny boots.

Their music was great, and you could tell they were having fun. They all had happy faces and laughing eyes.

We sat on one of the wooden benches, listened to the music, and looked around the plaza. We could see the old Spanish church that Dad said was built in 1706.

He said, "The church was called "San Felipe de Neri."

Like many of the old Spanish churches, it was a soft, light tan, almost cream color. It was built of adobe, and looked very inviting. Most of the buildings around the plaza were Spanish or Indian style, with flat roofs, and plastered adobe.

Dad said, "Albuquerque was settled by a wealthy Spaniard, who brought a few families with him. They started a cattle ranch here in Albuquerque. This entire plaza was a part of his ranch."

When we all got hungry we had an unusual treat. We ate at a restaurant. Like everything else here, it was Spanish. The inside had red brick floors, an open fireplace, and of all things, a real live tree growing up though the roof. That was very different.

There was a lot of pretty, blue tile throughout the eating area, and strings of red chili, called *ristras,* hanging on the walls. It was no fancy place. Blue jeans and cowboy boots were everywhere; however, cleanliness seemed to be the rule. It was so clean you could eat off the floor. It was quite pleasant.

We ate *frijoles* (beans), red and green chili, and *tortillas* (a flat, round, corn flour bread, cooked on a hot stove top). This was followed with fresh, cold milk. This was so much fun for us, as we never ate out. When we traveled, we had usually taken our food and our water with us. We would just get out of the car, find a nice place to sit, and eat outside.

After leaving the restaurant, we walked through a few of the shops, and then we had to move along, as we had a long drive ahead of us.

The closer we got to Roswell, the more the country changed. The Rio Grande River seemed to grow in width, and had turned a coco brown – not the clean, swift stream around the other areas where we had lived. The land had also changed. We were now in more of a desert area. The cotton wood trees, normally found in towns, and the mountain pines had become scrub brush and junipers. The soil became parched and barren. The sky had become a light blue, and wind blew stronger. A weathered silence enveloped us, as we drove for hour after hour. In the distance the sharp cutting mountains seemed threatening, and never ending. To me this seemed a barren wilderness. We passed town after town, but none of them were much different.

Sis and I got tired, and we slept a lot. We woke up when Dad pulled off the road to eat and sleep for a little while. It was a quiet, forsaken place and Dad warned us to look out for rattlesnakes.

He said, "Don't sit down in any cool place or around rocks without looking first. Snakes like those places as much as we do. Be careful."

Mama opened our lunch bag and gave everyone a sandwich, and some cut vegetables. We ate in silence, and just wanted to rest. When we finished eating, we had a good drink of water, and we all climbed back into the car, locked the doors, rolled down the windows a little bit, and all of us took a nap. Dad woke up first, and he drove on and on into the night.

Finally we arrived in Roswell. Dad had a house for us, and we went in, threw our sleeping bags on the floor. We all slept like logs. We were all exhausted.

The next day Dad went to work, and we went into our usual cleaning mode. This was probably the nicest house we had ever lived in, and I liked it. We made it as livable as possible, and it was not long before we got to know some of the local people. They all seemed to be nice, but they sure did talk a lot - even more than the card players had talked in the mountains. Politics seemed to be in the air. Every night when Dad came home, we listened to the news on the radio. There was constant talk about the unrest in Europe with Hitler's armies on the move.

Meanwhile, the weather was very hot, hotter than I had ever seen it. It was never this hot in the mountains. We had not been in Roswell very long when one day, on his day off, Dad said, "Come on, Sis, let's go and get some ice."

In the heat, ice sounded like gold, and I asked, "Where are we going to get ice, Dad?"

"Just come on. You will see."

Dad and I were the only ones to go. We drove a little ways out of town. He pulled over and parked, got a small hand pick and a gunnysack out of the car. We walked over to what appeared to be a giant hole in the ground.

Dad said, "See that ladder there. I am going to go down it. I want you to stay right here. You can sit in the car, but you are not to follow me for any reason. You're in the shade, so you will be fine."

"Is this where you are going to get the ice, Dad?" I asked thinking this could not be the place.

"Yes," he said. "People have been getting ice here for hundreds of years. I won't be to long. Are you going to be all right here?"

"Sure," I answered, trying not to show my misgivings.

I was so scared. I could not get my mind off Dad in that big hole. It didn't seem to bother him one bit though. The only thing that gave me comfort was not to think about where Dad was, and just remember the *mariachi band* at the restaurant, where we ate at Albuquerque.

Dad climbed down the old ladder. It looked like the Indian ladders that we had seen at the Pueblos. It made me very uneasy. I didn't like the idea of him going down into that cave.

It was not long, but it seemed like a long time to me, before Dad popped up, climbed out, and threw the sack on the ground and laughed. "Pretty cold down there," he said. "Come on, let's go home and make some ice cream."

When we got home Sis and Mama had the ice cream all mixed and ready to freeze. It was such good ice cream. The ice that was left in the sack was just thrown in the shade next to the house. Even at 114 degrees that ice lasted for three days.

When we had our first ice cream, one of our neighbors came over. He lived alone, and he liked to talk with Dad. His name was Nick Walters. Like always, politics soon came up. As we all ate our ice cream, we found out that he was working with Dad on the bridges. He did have a family, but they were living way up state, near Taos.

Nick told Dad that he had recently applied for Social Security. "That was the best thing that ever happened to this country. It feels good to put something away for your future. Some people have made a modest recovery, like you people, but there are still a lot of people who are in serious trouble, and it is not their fault."

He continued, "When you think about our history, you know this has always been a tough country with tough people. Take the Indians, then the Spaniards and Mexicans, and finally the White man. They came to a barren land, with little water, and they made a go of it. They learned to grow crops, learned to water and harvest them. They made cooking utensils. They learned to bake bread. They made cloth, rugs, and clothing. After all that, they started businesses. They were all very independent people. I often wonder how we got into such a mess as this depression. Maybe this 'Soak the Rich Tax' - you know the one that taxed the rich, and the profitable corporations more, the one that just passed in Congress, might just be a good thing. We just have to do something better. I know one thing for sure, I hate being away from my family. I think part of what has made this country great has been the strong families. I don't care what their nationality is. I don't care where they came from. It was the working man, who was the back-bone of this country."

"You are right there," Dad said. "It is just not right that some people have so much they don't know what to do with it, when the next fellow does not even have enough to eat, and no prospect of finding a way to take care of his family. Every worker needs to make a decent wage. If you don't earn enough to take care of your family, it isn't long before your entire country is in trouble. Most people don't want something for nothing. All they want is the opportunity to get ahead on their own. I don't know if I completely agree with these here isolationists, but I think we need to take care of our own people first, and what we all need is just the opportunity to work and to do that."

Mr. Walters nodded his head, shook hands with Dad, thanked Mama for the ice cream, and he went home to rest up for the long, hot, upcoming week.

Seeing the Country

One night after supper Dad said, "I think it is time for us to have a serious discussion. It looks like I will be working here for some time, so your mother and I decided that possibly we should give up the house in Bernalillo. If we do that, Sis can start school here, and we will just stay for as long as there is work here. What do you two think of that?"

"Great!" Sis and I both said, "But what about our trunk?"

"That is no problem. I had talked to Ricardo Pena sometime ago about doing something like this. He was open to the idea. All I have to do is let him know. He offered to take care of our things if we needed to leave them. Then he will rent the house. If we need the house later, we can rent it again if it is available."

"Now before you get excited about this, there are a few things to think about. First of all Sis will start school here when it starts. If I am moved, she may have to change schools, and that could possibly happen a number of times. Would that bother you, Sis?"

"No," she answered. "I would not mind changing schools. Anyway, I would rather us all stay together."

Dad said, "One advantage is that we will have a little more cash to work with if we are not renting two places to live. The disadvantage is that your Mama will have more work to do with all the moving and cleaning; however, Billy, you can hang around close to home and help Mama more. Now does anyone see any problems with this idea?"

"No," we all said. We liked the idea.

Dad said there was one more major thing he wanted us all to think about.

Mama said, "I'll tell them" Looking at us, she said, "Your father and I just wanted you both to know that probably some time soon, we will have a new baby."

Wow - I thought! "Where is the baby going to sleep, Mama?" I asked.

"Well, don't worry about that. We will figure out something when the time comes. Your father and I have been talking about one other thing. Go ahead and tell them, Bill."

"As long as we have been on the road, we actually have not done much as a family like we use to do. I thought now that we have a little more money, we can do more things together. I thought it might be nice when I am not working, for us to drive around some and see a few places of interest while we are traveling around the state. We have done a little bit of that, but not as much as I would like."

He took a breath and went on. "I know that this area is nothing like the area we have always lived in. It is different here, but if you look, it has a beauty all its' own. I know everything is very different. Instead of high, lush, ponderosa pines, fir, and spruce, you see bare, high mesas, *piñons* and junipers, miles of empty ground or sand dunes for as far as the eye can see. But you also see lovely miles of multi-colored desert with bold, bright sunsets - the most beautiful sunsets in the world. And the air is something else. No where do you breathe such clean, fresh air. It is almost as good as it is in the mountains."

"Where are we going to go, Dad?" Sis asked.

"Well, first I have to write Mr. Pena, and then I think it would be a good idea to start going someplace close."

Sand and Lakes

The first day we took a drive, we drove out of town, going to the southeast of Roswell. It was hot and dry, and Dad pointed out the prairie dogs. They were funny little animals. They sort of looked like a small rabbit, but stood, or rested their weight on their haunches, and looked at you. They had a face more like a cute little mouse, with smaller ears than rabbits, and close to their head. There were holes all over the ground, and Dad explained they had regular prairie dog towns under the ground. They would go into the holes, then pop right back out, or pop up out of the next hole. They made a funny noise, sort of like barking, but different. It was fun to watch them. Some times they just chattered to you.

Shortly we came to the Bottomless Lakes State Park. I asked Dad, "Why do they call them that?"

"They call them that because they have never found the bottom of them. No one has any idea how deep they really are. This entire area has miles and miles of caverns. Some of them are connected, and some are not. Someday we will probably know."

"Wow."

Dad drew our attention to the color of the water. It was the darkest water I had ever seen - light blue in some places, but most of it was a very dark blue, almost black in shadowy places. They were different than what we knew as lakes. It was very bare around them, mainly smooth rock. It seemed a long way down to where the water started.

"It is very pretty," Sis said. Mama agreed.

We walked around for awhile, found a nice place to eat our lunch, and after eating we started watching two horned toads. They were so funny. I asked Dad if I could pick them up and take them home. He told me to go ahead and pick them up, if I could.

First I felt them. They sort of felt like a frog, but they were different. I liked them better than frogs. They were quite rough and had what looked like a horn on their head. They looked like little, prehistoric animals. Sis and I put them in our bag and took them home.

We took very good care of the horned toads. We caught ants for them, and put weeds and greens in their box. We kept water in the box and kept them in the shade most of the time. We would take them out of the box, and have toad races.

Billy From Scratch

On Dad's next day off, we went for a drive to the northwest, into Lincoln County. Dad showed us where the infamous *Billy the Kid* had been in jail. He told us that his real name was *Bonney*. There were stories about him robbing banks, and killing. He was an outlaw. Dad said that there were stories that by the time he was twenty-one that he had killed twenty-one men. He said that once Judge Bristol, in the town of Lincoln, had sentenced him to hang, but he somehow escaped. He was eventually shot and killed by Pat Garrett. Garrett was the law, and had chased *Billy* for years. *Billy the Kid* was a young man when he died. Dad said he was buried just south of Ft. Sumner, New Mexico - that is about mid - central state, maybe about sixty miles west of the Texas border.

Dad told us that a lot of people thought *The Kid* was a hero, but Dad said he was not. It was said later that just about all the men he had killed, he had shot in the back. Dad said that didn't make a hero - it made him a "punk."

A Hot Summer

Summer labored on. It was hot, hot, hot, and dry. The wind blew and the sand was everywhere. We closed the windows, and the doors; however, the sand always found its' way in. It seemed like all we did was to clean up sand. It became a constant job.

Mama had more washing, as we were all going through more clothes.

At night Dad would come home, tired and hot. Sometimes when he got home, he would just sit under the shade tree, and drink water.

One evening after supper, our neighbor, Nick Walters, stopped by. He sat under the shade tree with Dad, and they pulled the radio outside and listened to the world news.

As usual, the news was grim. The newscaster said: "Employment continues to grow; however, unemployment is still quite high. Citizens had expected employment to rise rapidly due to the fact that Hitler had sent German troops into the Rhineland last March. Now Hitler offers France a twenty - five year, non - aggression pact. Neither France nor England seem to have any faith in Hitler's offer."

Dad turned the radio off.

"I suppose both countries doubted that pact would mean much of anything. Like the radio says, Hitler had lied time and again," said Mr. Walters.

Dad answered, "National elections will be coming in November. Let's just hope Roosevelt stays in office. I think it is essential that he is reelected. I hate to think of anyone getting into office that would concede more to Germany. I know that people want to believe Hitler because we don't want a war, but when you can't believe what a man says, you just can't trust him. Hitler makes promises, but they are worthless."

"I guess we are lucky to even have a job, Bill," said Mr. Walters. "The only complaint I have is that I don't get to see my family enough. My kids are going to think they don't have a father. I just don't like that. I think the world of that wife of mine, and my kids, and I want to be with them."

Mama patted Mr. Walters on the shoulder and said, "Nick, there are a lot of people still suffering from the depression, but we just have to keep plugging along until things get better. We know it is hard for you. I feel it is even worse when the entire world is in chaos. Try to keep your chin up."

Mr. Walters had such a sad look on his face. I think it took all of his attention not to cry. He hung his head, turned and waved as he walked home.

Dad's next day off was a trip for us to White Sands National Monument. It would be a pretty long drive. It had cooled off some, and we left early in the day. We drove southwest, going through Ruidoso, the Mescalero Indian Reservation, Alamogordo, and then we arrived at White Sands. By the time we got there, it was so very hot. Mama didn't seem to be feeling very well, so we stopped for awhile and had a cold drink from the water bag hanging on the front of the car.

Mama said she was fine and we better keep going, so we drove on. All you could see was sand.

After a short time Mama said, "Bill, I hate to be a spoilsport, but I think we better go home."

Dad looked concerned. He asked, "Are you feeling all right?"

"I don't feel very well. I feel all closed in with all this sand everywhere. I don't know - maybe I'm just claustrophobic, but I've never felt like this before. I don't like it."

Dad said, "It's all right, we're on our way home. As soon as we're out of this sand, we will stop, cool off, and have a nice drink of cold water. Just lean back and close your eyes. We will be home before you know it. Just sleep."

He found a place to turn around, and soon we were back on the road to Roswell.

Toward evening, when it cooled down and her nerves had settled, Mama was much better. She even ate a little bit.

"I'm sorry. I didn't mean to mess up your trip," she said.

"Don't worry about it, Mama," Sis said. "I don't like all that sand either. Besides, it is really hot. Maybe you better just rest tomorrow."

Mama went to bed early that night. Sis, Dad, and I went outside and sat on the front porch.

Dad said, "I don't like what happened to your mother today. I don't know if this is a good idea - Mama and you kids staying here. Maybe the heat and the travel are too much for her heart. Her color sure is not good."

"I could stay at home with her, and you and Billy could see what is around here," Sis said.

"No, that would not be fair for you. Let's just leave things alone right now, and see how Mama does. We can always change our plans down the road."

Schools – Disease – Poverty

It was time for school to start, and Sis registered at Roswell. It was a grade school that the WPA had built. Sis really liked it. She had a pretty, young teacher, and Sis enjoyed being in her class. The teacher explained things well, and she told the class that the New Mexico Military Institute was having a day that visitors would be allowed to tour the school.

After supper we talked about going to the Military Institute.

Mama said, "I don't see a reason in the world that we shouldn't go. It is right here in town - can't get much closer than that. We won't be gone for very long, and I think it is something we would all enjoy. Let's go."

We all liked that idea, and Dad didn't seem to worry about us going.

The day of the tour, we were all there. It was impressive. We were together in a group with other people, and when we were seated, an officer spoke to us before the actual ceremony started. He explained that the school offered high school, junior college, and also military training. After he finished talking, there was a military review. I never saw so much pomp and ceremony. You would swear it was actually full time military. Everyone was in uniform. They looked like they were ready for review in Washington, D.C. Every uniform was perfect. Every cadet was perfect. Every line was as straight as an arrow. The band played, and they marched in perfect unison. It was just so nice, and so military. It made you proud.

After the ceremony, we were all allowed to walk around and inspect the school. They served punch and cookies, and we did have fun.

As the weather cooled, Mama seemed to be better. Dad had taken her to the doctor. He told Dad and Mama that there was not much he could do for her. She had had rheumatic fever when she was thirteen years old. The doctor explained that as often happens, the heart valves were damaged, and since then there has been a gradual enlargement of the heart. He told Dad that with sensible activity Mama could live for some time. He offered nothing else.

On the way home Dad and Mama talked about the heart problem. Mama said, "I know it sounds grim, but it is not the end of the world. I know this doctor didn't tell us what we wanted to hear. Hopeless, or incurable, is a pretty grim analysis, but I don't think that necessarily means tomorrow. I'm sure there are many things you can do to help yourself. Nothing is going to keep you alive forever. Besides, there may be some natural things that help. Exercise can help, and eating right does amazing things. Let's not get discouraged about it. Let's just keep a positive attitude. You know attitude makes a big impact upon your life. Then of course, there is always prayer. Some say none of these things matter, but I have seen many people live where there seems to be no hope. I guess I believe there is always hope. Not only that, but passing away is out of our hands. Let's just live the best life we can and leave our dying to God. After all we have enough to think about that we can handle."

The Caves – The Big Boys

Life ambled on. Later in the fall there was a small group of people that were going to see the Carlsbad Caverns National Park, and I was invited because my friend had asked me to go with her. Dad said I could go if I stayed right with the group and didn't go away from them. He said before it was definite, I would have to check with Mama. She said the same thing Dad did.

The day we were to go Dad gave me some money for my admission and for food. We left very early in the morning, and my friend's mother drove. My friend's name was Mary Babcock, and she lived two houses from us.

I guess it was a long way, but the time went very fast. When we parked people were already lining up to follow the guide. Before we left, he checked to see how many were in the group - gathered us all together and talked to us before we started.

We were standing in the parking lot, and when we looked at the guide, we could see the big cave opening in front of us - just a little lower than where we were standing.

The guide said:

"The Carlsbad Caverns are the eighth Wonder of the World. They are world famous. The caverns were found when a cowboy, Jim White, saw the sky black with bats as they left the caves to look for flying insects for food."

"We will walk down a path, and it will be lighted. No one, under any circumstances, is to leave the path. When we have passed the entrance to the bat cave, the path divides. We will take the path to the right and go further down to a point where we will stop. When we stop, everyone is to squat down, and we will turn off all the lights. It will be the darkest dark you have ever seen. In a few minutes, we will turn the lights back on and proceed deeper into the caves. Now if there is anyone that does not want to go, this is the time to say so."

"Anyone?" he asked. No one left the group. The guide said there was one more thing: "No one is to touch either the stalactites - these are the cone-shaped formation building from the top, nor the stalagmites – coming up from the cavern floor. These caverns were made from water, one drop at a time, and taking millions of years to form. One fingerprint can stop the process and damage the rock. We do not know how long it would take to repair itself, if ever. So please, do not touch anything. This is very important. Are there any questions?"

There were no questions, and no one left the group. As we started walking down into the caves, additional guides joined our group, spreading themselves evenly among us.

I got the same strange feelings as I had when Dad went into the ice cave alone, but there was no way I would let anyone know how I felt. We walked and walked, and then I saw a lone bat flutter by.

The guide said, "Don't worry folks, they won't get near you. That is just a straggler coming in from last night. We probably won't see anymore of them. In the daytime, they usually sleep."

As we walked, the caves didn't look much different than other caves I had seen, but soon the path became steeper, and things started to look different. Off and on, other guides started explaining different things as we approached them.

"Notice the little pool on your left. That pool may be inches deep, or it may be hundreds of feet deep. That is one reason we must stay right on the path. Note the pretty color of it. Have you ever seen such pretty, deep blue?"

"Yes," I said to my friend, Mary. "When we went to the Bottomless Lakes, the water looked like this."

Shortly another guide said, "Let's all stop here for just a minute. Look up along the rock and see if you can see the anchors and the old ladders that the first explorers used to come into these caverns. You saw how dark it was when we turned the lights out. Can you imagine how hard it was for them to see with the sparse lighting they had? It must have been very difficult."

Soon we came to a wider area that looked like an apartment balcony. We looked down into what seemed like an enormous rock room. Here we actually saw the stalactites and stalagmites. They were absolutely beautiful. The colors were so delicate - browns, tan, cream, almost whites. There were places where they were so low that they could almost touch you. They were all different sizes. It was amazing how many different groups of rock there were - all different sizes, shapes, and beautiful, soft colors.

We slowly moved on down the trail, trying to take in all we were seeing. Some places the path narrowed so much that you had to turn sideways to pass through. Some places you had to bend down to keep the rock from touching you. Behind us an old woman said, "What if there was an earthquake now?"

"Oh, good grief, Mother," said her daughter.

Finally we were down in a large room ourselves. One of the guides told us that there were a number of these big rooms – actually, they had no idea of how many, nor of how many miles these caverns covered. Only about three miles were open to visitors. The guide said there would probably be more in time.

When we got to the big room, it was lunchtime, and there were tables, and benches. You could eat your own food, or you could buy food. Someone said that your own food tasted better, as the food in caves picked up a strange taste. The drinks did too. The caverns had a peculiar, musty smell.

We bought our food, and we ate. Then it was time to start the long walk back to the top. It was much harder going back up. I thought of Mama, and didn't think she could walk that much.

When we reached the top and were back in the parking lot, the guide told us that the gift shop had all kinds of information about the caverns, and he asked us to come back anytime. He said all Americans should see this wondrous place. He said this was one of our national treasures. I was glad that we had come.

We were so tired when we finished the day. Mrs. Babcock took us to a motel and we stayed for the night. Mary and I talked and talked. We would have even talked more about all we had seen that day, but we were so tired that we fell fast asleep.

Chapter 9

Moving On

When Dad came home from work, Mama knew something was wrong. She filled a glass of cold ice tea, and handed it to him. Then she sat down by him, under the shade tree.

"What is the matter?" she said.

"Nick Walters got killed today."

"Oh dear! How did it happen?"

"He got caught between two trucks, and he was crushed."

"That is terrible," said Mama. "What will happen to his family now?"

"Who knows? That is not all of it though. Work is moving. There will be a small cleanup crew left here, but the rest of us will start work next week at Grants. It is ironic isn't it? That move would have put Nick a fair day's drive closer to his family. That would have really pleased him. Remember when he said before, 'My kids will think they don't have a Dad.' Well, now they really don't."

"My heart just breaks for his family, said Mama. "I don't know that Nick ever said if his wife has any way to make a living to support that family!"

There was no talk for some time, and then Mama said, "I just heard on the news that the King of England had renounced the throne. He did it because he plans to marry that pretty, sophisticated woman, Mrs. Wallis Warfield Simpson. She must be some woman! It's so crazy though. It seems the only thing those Englishmen had against her marrying royalty was that she had been divorced. My, my, that sounds sort of uppity to me."

Dad said, "If you think about it, we have sort of the same thing here in our country right now. People seem to resent Mrs. Roosevelt going around the country, seeing what is going on, and talking to everyone. She's not a looker like Mrs. Simpson, but frankly, I think she is even presidential material."

"You're right there, but it will never happen - a woman?" Mama said. "However, she certainly is President Roosevelt's eyes and ears. What a lot of people do not realize is that she is needed, and she is doing a great job. Some people do not even know that the President is an invalid. Without her, he would never know what is really going on out in the work field. She was even down inspecting the coal mines, to see what the working conditions were there. I think she is incredible, but the President would have trouble doing that job without her."

Dad answered, "A lot of people thought Roosevelt could never win an election after he had polio, but he did. What some don't seem to realize, it was his legs that were paralyzed. There was nothing wrong with his head. When you think about it, Nick and his wife were in a similar situation. Two people can sometimes do a crack-up job together, but it is usually harder for one person, especially during times like this."

"I know," Mama said. "I just hope work really picks up more, and no one has to live like people are now - families divided, people starving. It has not been good for working people since the beginning of the depression.

For people like Nick, it has really been bad. I'm afraid, even if work gets better, it is going to be a real struggle for Nick's wife and his kids. I'll tell you what I think. I think it was smart for the King of England to give up the throne. I would pick family over being King any day; however, in Nick's situation, he had no choice."

Retracing Our Steps

We packed our meager belonging, and started north, retracing our steps along the Rio Grande River. When we got to Los Lunas, we turned west, and passed the Acoma Pueblo. Again, we could not stop. Dad had to be in Grants on Monday to start work, and we had to find a place to live before then.

As we backed tracked and headed north, we passed miles of dry, flat Indian Reservations. We were in Indian country. Any direction you looked, there was endless sand, with scrub juniper and piñon trees. In the distance, there were high, rough, sandstone bluffs, or deep gullies with sharp, high hills, where lava once flowed. Here and there, in the distance, you would see what looked like a blue mountain. That brought back to our memory the Sandia and the Jemez mountain ranges - green and lush, with fir, spruce, and pine trees. It made us feel just wonderful to see them even in the distance. We had always loved the mountains, but we were in desert area now. We all knew the views and types of land changed with altitude, and we were experiencing a big change now.

To break the long and tiresome drive, Dad would talk about the Spanish Bishop - Father Lamy, and we would talk about the places he passed when he walked this land. Every time there was some thing that we had read about in the book, we talked about it. Then Dad started telling us Indian stories, and about the history of the local Indians - the Pueblos, the Navajos, the Apaches, and the Comanches. He told us about the Anasazi, who had lived here thousands of years ago. He explained to us that the Anasazi had lived in the Grand Canyon many years before any other people lived in our area of the world. He said that Anasazi means the "Ancient Ones."

Finally we reached Grants. Dad went to the work office. He took care of his paper work, and the civil engineer told him there may be a few places to rent. He gave Dad the directions as to how to get to them. When we got to the area, there was one house available, but it was not much of a house, but we rented it. It was not nearly as nice as the house in Roswell, but it was big enough, and it was within walking distance of Sis's school. We moved our meager possessions in, and the cleaning process started again.

Sis started school. The next big event was the arrival of my Grandmother. She had come to help Mama when the new baby came. Shortly after Grandmother came my new brother arrived. There was much discussion after he was born as to his name.

Mama said, "Well Bill, now that we have already used your name, what are we going to name his new young man?"

Dad rubbed his head and answered, "It has to be a good name, a name that stands for something. We will give him a fine name."

Mama just waited.

Dad said, "I think I would like to name him Grant, not after this town, but after my favorite relative. You know I was closer to him than I was to any of my relatives. I knew him better, and I saw him more. He was more like a brother. My uncle was a fine man."

A tear ran down Mama's cheek and she smiled and said, "I think that is a fine idea. His name is Grant."

With that settled life went on as usual. It was so much fun having Grandma at our house, but slowly a problem began to develop.

I had not decided about my new brother yet. He was little, and red. It seemed like he cried a lot and anytime he did, everyone ran. Everyone said how proud my Dad must be to have a son. Sometimes they would say indelicate things like, "Oh, it is too bad you already used the name Billy. It is nice to name a son after his father."

"Well", I thought to myself, "it's not so bad to name a daughter after her Dad either." It then entered my mind, "I just don't know if I am going to like this kid or not." Then I had worse thoughts, "Is Dad going to take him fishing instead of me? Is he going to read stories to him, and just forget about me and Sis?" All kind of thoughts entered my mind.

One day as I was struggling with this new problem, my Grandmother came and sat down beside me on the front steps. She said, "What do you think about this new brother?"

I answered, "I don't know. He is little, and sort of cute in a way, but what do think Dad thinks about him?"

"I thought you might have that on your mind," she answered. "Did you know that I had six children?"

"No."

"Well, I did, and I will tell you about the most wonderful miracle? The miracle is that it does not matter how many children you have, you love every one of them."

"What if you had ten?" I asked.

"It doesn't matter. You can have twenty. You see that is what the miracle is. Every child that is born brings something very special into this world. There are never two that are exactly the same - not even if they are identical twins. Everyone has special things about them. You see your Dad sees special things in you, and he loves you for them. He will also see special things in your new brother, and he will love him also. He may, or may not, treat him the same, but he will love you both, and there is even love left over

113

for Sis, and for Mama. Love is a strange thing. The more you love people, the more they love you back, and it just keeps spreading. Now what do you think about that, Little One?"

"I think that sounds OK, Grandma."

Grandma smiled, and said, "I think maybe we will leave that new baby for Mama to rock, and we could skip a little rope. What do you think? I think I can beat you."

"Oh, I don't know, Grandma!" I can jump rope pretty good. "Let's call Sis, and we will see who wins!"

Life at Grants

Life was so fun with Grandma. One night just before Dad got home, and Grandma was cooking supper, a very drunk Indian man just walked into our living room. Mother was rocking the baby, and Grandma just walked over to the Indian and told him he was in the wrong house. At the same time, she turned him around and walked him right out of the front door. We never saw the man anymore. He never showed up again at our house.

He was so funny. We just laughed and laughed. We always wondered what house he finally ended up in. We just hoped he had gotten home.

Every day that Grandma was at our house was wonderful. She was never ending fun. We jumped rope quite often. It was hard to beat Grandma. Sis and I really had to work on that. Whenever Sis or I won, Grandma would say, "Well, you beat me this time but just wait until tomorrow." She quite often won.

Since we moved to Grants, there were more kids to play with. Some of them came from the school where Sis went. Some of them were Mexican kids that sometimes didn't go to school. Some of them were Indian kids that were too young to go to school, or were home from school, because of different reasons. Most of the Indian kids went away to special Indian schools, where they usually stayed all the school year, except for a few special occasions.

Most of the time there were enough kids for a good baseball game. We had lots of vacant area to play in, and someone always had a bat and ball. We even had them. We had good games. Everyday we would hurry to get our work done so we could go play ball. Sis was often the pitcher, but I liked to play short-stop.

Sometimes we would play other games. We played one game where we drew straws. The person with the shortest straw was "it". That person would count to ten, and then kick the can. Everyone else would run and hide, while the kicker again counted ten. Then the person, that kicked the can, starting looking for kids hiding. If they spotted one, both would run to kick the can again. Whoever reached the can first, and kicked it, won. Then they could go and hide, and the other person was "it". We played that game for hours. We had a lot of fun.

We played games that we had just made up, or versions of old games that our parents and even grandparents had played when they were young – games like: anti-anti over, hop-scotch, and a lot of other children's games.

This was the first time that Sis and I lived around enough other children to actually play team sports. In the mountains, or even in Roswell, we never played baseball as a team. When Sis and I played ball, it was just the two of us, with one of us hitting and the other one catching.

All of that changed when Grandma came. She would go out with us to play. If she saw someone watching, she would call out, "Hi, do you want to come play ball?"

Most of the time they did, and soon we had enough for two teams. We were an odd mixture of kids. We were all ages. We had a wonderful time. The Mexican kids knew the game well, and were usually good players. The Indians were the best runners. They could run like a deer and never seemed to get tired. Sis and I were among the few white faces, and most of us were just learning the game, so we all had to work hard at it, but in time we all held our own. One good thing about baseball is that everyone can be a hero. All you have to do is to hit a home run. Baseball had become a fun game for us, and a lot of the other kids.

The Eagle

One day when Dad came home from work, he was carrying a dead eagle. He told us that someone had shot it, and he found it close to where he was working.

"What are you going to do with it, Dad?" I asked.

He said, "We are very close to the big Navajo Reservation here, so I think I will give it to one of their people. I may know someone there. The Indians a have high regard for the eagle. I am sure that they would appreciate it."

"Can I go with you, Dad?" I asked.

"No, Sis, not this time. Maybe you can go some other time."

Dad carefully spread the eagle out, and wrapped it in a clean rug. Then he left the house and he was gone for a long time.

The next day was a school day, and there were not enough players for a baseball game, so Grandma and I were just sitting on the steps watching the sky.

I asked, "Grandma, why did Dad take the eagle to the Indians?"

"Honey, your Dad was born in Colorado, and he has lived there, or in New Mexico, all of his life. He has spent a lot of time with Indians. He thinks well of them and although he does not always agree with all of their thinking, he respects them and their beliefs. Over the years, he has learned much about how they think, and what is important to them and what is not. He understands the basis of their religion - although they share very little of what their beliefs are. The Indian people have a close relationship with all living things, but even more important they have a strong attachment and respect for the land - the earth it's self. They call the earth 'Mother'. They closely tie their strength to their ancestral lands where they were born and where they live. They felt these same lands were shared with ancient ancestors and they considered them all sacred places. I think that the Indians still believe that the actual spirits of their ancestors inhabit these wild, beautiful lands. The people living today still feel responsible to these ancient ones who had preceded them in death."

Grandma thought for a moment. We were both thinking and quiet for sometime, and then she continued, "I guess maybe the closest thing I can think of is that the Indians looked at the land itself somewhat as the White Man looks at his church. When the Spanish came into this area, they tried to convert the Indians to their religion. The Indians were agreeable to going to the Spanish churches; however, I don't think there was ever any thought of giving up their own beliefs as far as religion. This later became a big issue – both to the White Man and to the Indian. I think your Dad explained some of this to you when he gave you your book. If you ask him, I am sure he will explain more. He knows more about it than I do."

I was temporarily satisfied with Grandma's explanation. Anything else I could learn from her would have to wait. It was time for Grandma and me to go back into the house and start doing some cooking. Mama was gaining strength and little brother was getting so cute. When you tickled his belly, he would laugh. I decided he was pretty good after all. "Grandma," I said, "I guess maybe we better keep him."

Grandma just bent over laughing.

Finally the day came that Grandma had personal business to take care of at her home, so she had to leave us. When she left we put her on the train and she hugged us all, and said, "Now you watch for nuts every now and then. When the pecans are ready, I will send you a box through the mail." Looking at me she said, "And young lady, it will be your job to shell them when Mama needs them. Can you do that?"

"Yes I will do that, but I wish you didn't have to go home. We had so much fun with you."

After Grandma left our life went on much as it had before. Dad was still working in the area. Sis was doing well in school. I was always working on my reading. My little brother, Grant, was growing. Mama was better at times and worse at other times. We were eating a little better, but we still never had any extra money. Times were still pretty hard for most working people. All of our friends that we kept in touch with were experiencing about the same problems that we were. The depression had hurt many good people.

One Saturday morning, Dad asked me, "Sis, do you still want to go to the Indian Reservation?"

"Oh yes," I answered.

Dad said, "We will actually be going deep into the Indian Reservation and you will need to stay with me at all times. You can listen all you want to – but no talking, except to answer a direct question. If you want to know something, or ask any questions, you will have to wait until we are back in the car, and on our way home. If you can do that, you can go. What do you want to do?"

"I can do that, Dad. Sure, I want to go with you," I answered.

"OK," Dad said, "Let's go."

As we drove, Dad pointed out snowcapped Mount Taylor, which is a very old volcano. Grants sets right at the base of this lovely blue mountain peak. As we went by, Dad pointed out things to me -"this is a good place to go in the summer to get out of the heat. Do you see where the tree line changes from juniper and piñon to spruce? Those areas right up there are full of deer and elk, and there is an abundance of growth and wild life. Look higher up there. See the different color? That is where the big ponderosa pines grow. You can often see mountain sheep up there, bear and the mountain lion. That is where you will find the eagle. That, Sis, is the king of all birds."

"Is that why you gave the Indians the eagle you found, Dad?" I asked.

Dad answered, "I guess you would say I gave it to them because I know they put great value on the eagle. Indians are very private about what they think and believe, especially things that are of great importance to them. They share their thoughts with very few people, and hardly ever with strangers. From what I know of the Indians, the eagle is some kind of important symbol to them. I've never been able to pin down exactly what they believe regarding the eagle, but I feel it has something to do with the spirits of their ancestors. I may be completely wrong, but I guess, what really matters is that they are completely in awe of them. They seem to have a reverence, and great esteem for the eagle."

We drove along in silence for a long time. Now and then Dad would point his finger at one thing or another, and tell me things about it. We drove west past Gallup, then turned northwest, in the direction toward Shiprock and Farmington. After some time Dad turned off onto a rough narrow trail of a road. Dad told me that to the east was the Coyote Wash, and a little north of that was the Chaco River, but we were going more to the northwest into dry, desert country. This was country of sand colored plateaus - dry, tablelands, also called mesas. There are high rock formations, rattlesnakes, burros, yucca, sparse water, and arroyos, which are dry gullies, which run fast and high after desert rains.

We slowly moved along the rough trail. Finally I asked, "Dad, why do these Indian houses look different than the ones in the Jemez Mountains and Bernalillo? They are really different than Taos."

"The reason is that we are looking at different people. Sure, they are all Indians, but just like the White Man, or any other race, there are differences. See, the Indians that lived in the Grand Canyon area originally were Pueblos. They were 'cliff dwellers', and eventually became the big pueblo builders. Indians here on this reservation are mainly Navajos. When the Navajos came they were a war like people that moved with the seasons and they followed the buffalo. They were a transitory people. The Pueblos were a farming group and lived mainly where there was enough water. That is one reason why their houses and villages are different. The Navajos moved quickly with their lifestyle. For a long time they lived in tents, while the Pueblos stayed more or less in the same areas. The Pueblos built larger more permanent buildings. You see different people have different needs, so they build different kinds of building - building that suit their different needs."

Dad said, "This is where we are going, Sis. This is where Running Bear lives. Now remember, I told you before, let me do the talking. Don't forget."

An old, wrinkled Indian man came outside to greet us. He stood straight as an arrow. He had clear sharp eyes, and he motioned for Dad

to come in. At the same time he called to the big, menacing dog to lie down and be quiet. The dog obeyed immediately.

Dad came and opened my door and said, "Just quietly walk along with me and stay close."

We went inside and it took a few minutes for our eyes to adjust to the darkness. The only light came from the open door. When we could see, we sat on a lovely Navajo rug - one we would think would be too good to put on any floor, especially a dirt one. Running Bear sat across from Dad, and I sat next to Dad. Now, I looked around me. To one side of the one -

room house, there was a loom, with a half-finished Navajo rug in the process of being made. On the other side were three racks holding fabulous finished rugs. One strange thing I noticed was that there were few people around.

Dad and Running Bear started talking, sometimes in Spanish, sometimes in Indian, and occasionally in English. I could not follow what they were talking about, and I sat quietly. In time Running Bear handed my Dad a pipe, and Dad smoked, and handed the pipe back. They continued smoking and talking for a while, and finally Dad stood up, as did Running Bear.

Running Bear walked to a side shelf that I had not noticed, and picked up a small, leather drum, and handed it to me.

Dad said, you can say "Thank you."

"Thank you," I said, and smiled at Running Bear.

Running Bear said something to Dad, but it was in his language and I could not understand.

We all walked out of the door, and again Running Bear quietly spoke to the dog. We got into the car, waved, and drove away.

After we had driven awhile, I asked, "Dad, where were all the people? I didn't see hardly any."

"Running Bear was there to meet with us. Most everyone else was busy. Some of the children are away at school, and everyone else is working. There is a lot of work to do before winter, so everyone must help. Every tribe's survival depends on the families working together. I think sometimes we could learn a lot from the Indians."

"It was very nice of Running Bear to give me this drum. It is made of real leather isn't it?"

"Yes, it is Sis, and very well made. He gave it to you because he thinks you are a good child. I think he likes you. He gave you a compliment.

"Well, I like him too," I answered. "I will always take very good care of this drum."

We quietly bumped along the rough trail for a while, and I thought of another question. "Dad, why do the Indians keep that mean dog? He is big, and he is pretty, but he scares me."

Dad chuckled, and said, "Sis, that dog is actually a wolf. The Indians have quite a lot of them. The more you are in Indian villages, the more you will see them."

It didn't take long before I had another question. "Dad, how did you get to know Running Bear?"

"Now that is a long story, Sis. Maybe someday I will tell you that story, but not today. The long and short of it is that he saved my life, and another time, I saved his. I have known him for many years. In fact, I guess you could say that Running Bear and I are like blood brothers."

Party Time

Uncle John, Aunt Margaret, and Little John came to our house. Uncle John's work was moving and he was going to work near Bernalillo. Dad would also go there so we would be living close to them again soon. We were thrilled. We were looking forward to their company.

In addition to that good news, there was one other thing that made us excited. The working cowhands had just driven in a herd of cattle to be loaded onto railroad cars and sent to the East. Everyone knew the meaning of that - a big party!

Everyone knew there would be a free, impromptu rodeo. There would be bronco busting, lassoing, wild bull riding, bareback riding, and steer wrestling. The best cowboys in all events would be judged. Their skills would essentially be determined on every degree of riding, and all their learning and experience; however, since they had spent many months on the range working cattle, they were wild and full of vinegar. They were ready to test the livestock and their skills to the limit. People that didn't have enough money to buy groceries would bet on their dare - devil riders. The competition would be wild, reckless, rough, and ferocious. These cowboys were out to win, and the cost was not to be considered.

Some of them would win a small pot fed by the betting proceeds as a prize; however, that was not the prize they were risking their necks for. The big prize was the honor of being judged "the best."

After the rodeo, there would be a big street dance. The cowboys had a little money in their pockets, and most of them were throwing it away. They would drink and eat, and play cards. They would just have a good time, and the party would probably last most of the night.

The day the cattle reached the rail head the air was electric. There was a feeling of excitement throughout the entire area. Men started working getting the area ready for the rodeo. There were fences to put up, and chutes to pull out. At the yards the cattle were being loaded, and everything came to life. At our house Mama and Aunt Margaret started cooking.

After supper Dad and Uncle John caught up on their missed political talks, and Dad asked Uncle John if he had heard anything from Matt and Rita – our old friends from the mountains.

"The last thing I heard of them," said Uncle John, "was that they were doing pretty good. Their ranch was growing and they were getting a good sized herd of beef cows. That's about all I know about them."

As the women worked, the men watched the town activity and Uncle John asked Dad what he thought about the war news from Europe.

Dad answered, "I heard that Hitler had recently assumed complete control of all of the German armed forces, and there are rumors that he also gave himself the power to shoot anyone who disagrees with him. There is no doubt that he is power hungry, but he really is a madman. What have you heard?"

"I understand that England and France are trying to reason with him, but I don't think that will change anything. It doesn't seem to me that Neville Chamberlain has the talent for the job of Prime Minister," said Uncle John. "You know the Foreign Secretary, Anthony Eden, resigned because of Chamberlain's policies. Eden seemed to size up Hitler a long time ago. He sees that Hitler is playing a game – give a little, then back down a little, but keep gaining what you want until you can take the whole enchilada. A lot of the world sees it like that too, and it keeps a great deal of people in a state of anxiety over Hitler's radical, self - serving policies. I don't think that there is any doubt that we will be in war before very long."

"I'm afraid your right there, John," answered Dad. "I do think things are getting a little better here though. We've had our ups and downs, but more people are getting back to work again. There is still a lot of fighting in Washington about the financial troubles of the railroads. A lot of people in government think there should be more consolidation to save costs. The current efforts are to work out a permanent solution. As far as we are concerned, work is pretty good right now, but there is still a lot of moving around. It is still pretty good around Bernalillo, so we will probably be there for awhile."

That night we all went to bed late, and got up early the next day. We wanted to get to the rodeo early to find a good place to watch. We knew there would be a lot of people there. There were no bleachers at all, so we found a good place right next to the fence, and threw our blanket on the ground.

Dad said, "Now you guys all keep your eyes open, and if one of those wild critters come this way, jump up and get behind this truck here. You don't want one of those babies running over us."

The rodeo started on time, and it was a blast. There was a campfire a short distance behind the chutes, where the animals came out. The cowboys where standing around and they had a big pot of coffee over the fire. You could tell they were all fired-up and ready to go. Some of them wore chaps, but most of the boys took them off, and rode without them. When they called their name, the rider stood up, pulled their hats down over their eyes, and strutted over to the chutes like they had already won the prize.

I really liked the wild bull riding. When the chute was open, the bull came charging out, and the cowboy was hanging on for dear life. Up and

down both of them went. Most of the cowboys were thrown off in no time flat. Then it was time to get up, and get out of the way of the bull. The bull would run right after them, and the clowns would have to distract them. The cowboy got out of the ring as quick as possible. Finally, one of cowboys stayed on for the full time. The next problem was to get him off before he broke his neck. Before the bull riding was over, we had three cowboys stay the time, and then the first winner was decided. He was a tall, thin, young man, with a twinkle in his eye, and he threw his hat in the air, and yelled, "Yeehaw!" He made us laugh and we liked him a lot.

There was one event right after another. Noon came so fast, we could not believe it. We ate our sandwiches, and kept watching. I thought the next most exciting thing was the saddle *bronc* riding. Those broncos didn't want to be ridden, and they didn't co-operate one bit. In this event, one of the cowboys was thrown off, and the bronco got right after him. When they got the half-wild horse distracted, they had to carry the cowboy off to be attended to. Later, it was announced that he had a broken arm, but he did come back and wave to the crowd with his good arm.

At four o'clock in the afternoon, the rodeo was still going full blast. Everything was so good, and the cowboys had a wonderful time, as well as the spectators.

As dark approached, the rodeo was finally over. The winners all came inside to the front of the judging stand and received their awards. Everyone stood and gave them a big hand. Then the money was divided according to the amount each should get, and it was all over until the next herd arrived. It was the most fun day we had had in years. Little John threw her arm around my shoulder, and said, "You'll never know how much my family and I have missed you guys. I'm so glad that we will be seeing more of you now."

We ate supper at home. We had boiled beans and warm cornbread, with fresh applesauce. We watched the dancing from the front steps, but we did not leave the house. Everyone was all tired out so we all went to bed early. We had to start getting ready to move the next day. We would be going back to Bernalillo again. We expected our life would be much the same as it was before, when we lived there; however, now we would have our very best friends living close to us. We all liked that idea.

Chapter 10

Back to Bernalillo

Dad had already written Ricardo Pena about renting his house again. Mr. Pena told Dad that it had just been vacated, and we were welcome to take it. So that is where we went.

The renters had left the house pretty clean, so we had less work cleaning, and moving in was easy, since we did not have much to move. Mr. Pena had kept our things, and every thing was in perfect condition. When we were settled, it seemed like we had not even moved, although we had been away for a number of years. It was so nice to stretch-out on the floor again on the bear rug, and look into the bear's mouth and run our fingers over the bear's teeth. At night, I would stretch out on the rug, and I started reading my book again. It was just like it was a new story. We talked about it a lot. Dad said it was true and there was a monument to Kit Carson between Albuquerque and Santa Fe. He was a real person. He was the famous Indian scout in my book, and he was a good friend of Father Lamy.

Uncle John and his family found a house just a couple of blocks away. By the time we were settled in Bernalillo, it was time again for school to start. Little John was registered to go to the public school. Since Sis had done so well here before at the Catholic school, Dad and Mama decided we would both go to that school. That was old hat for Sis, but since I was just seven and starting school for the first time, it was all new to me. When we went to school, Sis and I walked in one direction, and Little John went in another.

The Catholic School consisted of two buildings. Both buildings were two-story, and built of block. The boys were in one building, and the girls in the other. Brothers taught the boys, and the girl's building was located across the street, and about a block away, and the classes were taught by nuns. My teacher's name was Sister Mary Rose. She was old, grouchy, and very strict.

Sis made friends very easily, and always had someone to walk to school with. Usually I would just follow along behind her. One day Sis and her friend had gotten far ahead of me, as I was dawdling pretty far behind when I reached the boy's school. A big, ugly, red-headed, condescending boy threw a rock at me, and said, "Where you going, Beanpole?"

I just kept walking, and tried to ignore him. I went on to school and didn't say anything about it to anyone.

The next day, he was waiting for me again. This time Sis was with me, and he didn't say anything.

This set a pattern. If I was alone, he would taunt me. If Sis was with me, he would make hand signs to me, if she couldn't see him. He would stick out his tongue, and act silly. Still, I tried to ignore him.

One day I was alone. He was waiting and was very obnoxious. He called to me, "Hey kid, don't you have any shoes better than those? Why do wear those clodhoppers? You look like a skinny boy - short kinky hair, boy's boots, you're a bean-pole. I'm going to beat you up one of these days!"

I was mad. He didn't know anything about me at all. Why is he doing this?

One day, when I got to school, I didn't feel good at all. Sister Mary Rose sent me home, and told me to come back when I was better.

When I got home, Mama called the doctor. He came right away. He looked at me and asked, "Does she have a rash?"

Mama and the doctor both looked me over good. It took little time to spot the tiny, red clusters of blistering. He looked in my mouth, "No rash here," he said. "But there isn't always a rash in the mouth. It looks to me like she has shingles."

"Shingles?" questioned Mama. "How would she get them?"

"I don't know," answered the doctor. "They are highly contagious. Usually a person gets them when they have a low immunity, or have been under a great deal of stress. Has she?"

"A few years ago she ran a nail right through her foot, and then we moved a lot after that. I can see where there would be stress, first with the foot, and then the big changes in her life; however, I don't know that she was exposed to anything."

"Well shingles are caused by a virus. Sometimes a person is exposed, and does not even know it for years. When there comes a time of difficulty in their life, the virus can become active and that in turn causes an irritation of the nerve endings. The virus is kin to smallpox. She will be sick for awhile."

The doctor said, "Keep her in bed and give her lots of fluids. Cover those rashes with a clean, white cloth. You can put a baking soda paste on them. They will be very itchy. I'll leave her some medicine, and most important, keep her isolated. She is highly contagious right now. I'll drop in again, and if you see any signs of trouble, just call me. I'll be glad to come back."

The doctor was right. The itching was troublesome, and continued day and night. Sometimes it actually hurt. When Mama changed the bandages, they were bloody, stinky, and sometimes stuck to the bandage, and *hurt* when they were removed.   I thought I would never get over this awful thing.

The Conflict

When Mama found out I was so contagious, she sent Sis and Grant away to stay with Uncle John and Aunt Margaret, and I couldn't see Little John until I wasn't contagious anymore.   I read my book, and ate whatever Mama gave me, and I just hated being in bed. But finally it all passed, and I was able to return to school.

By the time I went back to school, Sis had made new friends and she walked to school with them.   I walked the two miles by myself.   It was not long before that disgusting, obnoxious, red-headed kid was back at it again pushing me around.

I had only been back in school about a week or so, when he confronted me on the way to school. This time he was out of the school fence, and waiting for me. I tried to avoid him, but again he threw a rock at me, and hit me right in the face. I bled like a pig.

Anger welled up inside of me, and I chased him. He slipped and fell, and I jumped on top of him with both feet. I grabbed a heavy stick that was right beside us, and beat the living daylights out of him. When he tried to get up, I grabbed him by the hair, and hit him right in the face. Then I threw the stick down and ran to school.

Sister Mary Rose looked at me when I walked into the building. She stood with her hands on her hips, and said, "Come with me to the office."

When I went into the office she said, "You don't have to bother telling me what happened. I have been notified so I know. I understand you attacked little Henry Franklin, and broke his nose. Is this true?"

I shrugged my shoulders. I didn't know that I had broken his nose.

She asked nothing else, and said, "Put your hands on the table, with your palms up." She then proceeded to hit my hands with her ruler.

When she stopped she said, "Now you go to the girl's room, and clean yourself up. I will notify your parents, and I never want anything like this to happen again. Go!"

I felt so bad. All I wanted to do was to go back to the mountains, and get away from these awful people. I really didn't like the idea of Sister Mary Rose telling my parents that I was bad. I really didn't think I was bad. Whatever happens, I knew one thing, I would never cry, no matter what Sister did to me. Henry had no business hitting me, and I was not sorry.

When I got home from school, Mama saw me and asked me what happened. I told her everything. I never saw her so mad. She told me to stay in the house until Dad got home, and she picked up Grant and they went to school. I never knew what she told Sister Mary Rose, but I knew after that that Sister never liked me; however, she never touched me again. She did keep me after school though – everyday until the other kids got home.

The day it happened, Dad had not been home long when Mr. Franklin, with Henry in tow, knocked on our front door. Dad answered.

"Yes," he said.

Mr. Franklin said to Dad, "Do you know that Billy beat my son up on the way to school? He knocked him down, and when he tried to get up, he broke his nose."

"Really," said my Dad. "We'll have to get this straightened out!"

Then he called me, "Billy, come here."

I walked in, and said, "Yes, Sir."

Mr. Franklin had a strange look on his face. He looked at me, and his eyes caught Henry's.

Looking at Henry, Dad said, "Did you have a fight with this young man today."

"Yes, Sir," I said again.

Mr. Franklin looked at me, took in my size, looked at my bruised face, then he looked at Henry, and his face turned red. He grabbed Henry by the collar, turned, and pulled him home. We never saw Mr. Franklin again, but Henry never bothered me again.

After Mr. Franklin and Henry left, Dad bent over laughing. When he caught his breath he said, "Sis, you did a pretty good job on that kid, but I think he probably deserved it. I want you to remember one thing though, never be a bully; but, on the other hand, never let anyone bully you either." Then he mussed my hair, and we sat down at the table for supper.

From that time on, things were somewhat better for me. Sis continued to get straight A's, and my grades were acceptable. Sister Mary Rose always treated me as if she was mad at me. Maybe it was because of my fight with Henry, or maybe it was because I could read and tell time. She did not like it when I already knew what she was teaching. One thing I knew for sure, she didn't like me. Often in class, she would call me a bad girl, and I think most people believed it, because she always kept me after school.

One day when the subject came up at home Dad said, "Just don't get upset over what Sister says. Just do as good as you can. Maybe what is wrong with Sister has nothing to do with you. She just seems to be an angry person to me. Try to remember, we know when we do right or wrong. It is perfectly all right to stand up for what you know is right. It doesn't matter what other people think, just like Sister Mary Rose. I think in her case, she never bothered to check the facts. People do that sometimes, you know."

Dad continued, "You know you were attacked, and you know you did all you could to avoid it. Let Sister choose to believe whatever she chooses to believe. You can't control that, and you did try to explain, but she chose not to listen. As far as her calling you a bad girl, we know that is not the truth. You're a good girl, and never let anyone put you down. You don't have to believe what other people say. It seems to me that people always have their own agenda. We can all just forget about what Sister has done. Keep doing your best, and know that your family thinks well of you."

A New Life

My year in the second grade was uneventful. I had a lovely new teacher. She was a young nun by the name of Sister Loretta. She was wonderful, and I liked her very much. She would let me read stories to the class, and she never kept me after school.

We got a new baby sister at our house, and Sister let me tell the class all about her. She had very white skin, and very black hair, and a lot of it. Pretty soon it all came out and she had no hair at all. She was a bald-headed baby, but we liked her anyway.

Uncle John, Aunt Margaret and Little John were still living close to us, and we saw them often. Dad and Uncle John still talked about what was going on around the world.

One night after supper, Dad and Uncle John were talking about war threatening Europe. Dad said, "Probably the whole world will be in it, if it actually starts."

They both knew that early in the year, President Roosevelt had made an appeal to Hitler for peace. Hitler rejected that appeal, and tried to turn the truth around by taunting our president, and everyone else who opposed him. He ordered the German high command to prepare to attack Poland. That was all people talked about. Everyone was in a state of agitation. Many were upset and thought we would go to war.

With the possibility of our country being attacked, our economy started to get better. People had great faith in President Roosevelt, but more and more people started to prepare their families to survive during wartime. Then one day when Dad had an extra three cents in his pocket, he bought a current newspaper when he came home from Bernalillo. The headlines screamed at us:

September 1, 1939

HITLER'S ARMIES ON THE MOVE
POLAND IS ATTACKED
WAR

Every newspaper in the land carried similar headlines. War was all anyone talked about. The first time Dad saw Uncle John, he said, "That was a real blow last Friday, when the paper came out." He looked upset, and even angry as he asked Dad, "Well Bill, after the last world war, did you ever dream we would be on verge of another world war? Now that the German army has attacked Poland, do you even think there is a possibility of them stopping?

"No."

Uncle John nodded his head, and said, "Hitler has been trying to sell himself as a friendly, caring man, who is dedicated to the care and good of the German people, but it seems he tends toward war and power. What do you really see in that man?"

Dad rolled his eyes, and answered, "That is a hard question. Some people think he is a genius, and follow him blindly. But you know what the other side of a genius is. I think he lives in a fantasy. When you hear him speak, or read what he says, and compare it with what he does, a dark picture is starting to develop. From the things he has changed in Germany, and from what he says, makes me think he wants to conquer the world."

John perked up, "What do you mean? What changes?"

Dad answered, "There are a number of things. He appears to be an artist at propaganda. When he speaks, he is careful not to disclose his shrewd plans until he has the actual power to follow through with them. The invasion of Poland is a perfect example of that. When he does move, he is vicious. If you look back to his climb to power, you see a vile degenerate. Another thing, he makes all kinds of promises. Just look at the treaties he has broken, and how often he tells a fellow leader something, then he does just the opposite. He never keeps his word. What bothers me most is that people don't seem to see what he is doing."

Uncle John rubbed his chin and said, "You know that is all true. For a long time England and France have been telling us that news has been suppressed, and very strictly enforced. It seems you only hear what news the party allows."

Dad added, "I've heard that about restricting news also. Another thing that bothers me is that Hitler knows how to play on people's emotions. If you notice when he talks, there are always props - there are red flags with swastikas. The Nazi party symbol is all over the place in full view. One more thing jumps out at me. I've noticed he completely disregards the facts, and he certainly hammers repetition. He seems to think if he positively states anything enough times, it is the truth. I am afraid we might just have a fanatic with too much power in his hands. It could be a travesty."

John said, "I guess it does not matter what we think, it is something we will have to deal with one way or another. We will see changes very rapidly now. For sometime England has been making preparations. Reservists have already been called to serve. School children have been sent out of the cities for safety. They have used everything for defense possible. Even old people, who can barely walk, have been issued pitchforks to defend England."

"In this country, President Roosevelt has already warned Americans to stay away from danger zones. If anyone is caught in Nazi controlled areas, they may not get out," Dad added. "I think very soon you will see alliances shifting around. I'm sure Canada will stick to England's side. Russia is still a wild card. Who knows which way they will go. I'm sure Italy will go with Germany."

"Well, so be it," said Uncle John. "Time will tell, and in the meantime, we better do all we can do to plan ahead. Right now, let's just enjoy this beautiful day, and then go have supper."

"John, before we go into the house to eat, there is something I want to tell you."

"What is it?" asked Uncle John.

"I've put in an application for a railroad job. I think there is a pretty good chance of getting it. If I do get it, we will be moving. I don't think it will be before next summer, or maybe even in the fall. I'll take it if I get the chance. It will be a good job, and with war on the horizon, I can't see there not being any work there for years to come. Don't say anything yet to anyone. There will be a lot of people trying for it. I don't want to get the family excited until I know for certain I have the job."

John said, "Bill, we have been friends for a long time. We'll all miss you and your family if you go, but I would never do anything to hold you back. We won't be that far away, and we'll still see you. I hope you get it. Good luck, fella."

The school year flew by. Everything went well, and we enjoyed Uncle John and his family. Little John was my best friend, and we had a lot of fun. I always found something interesting in school. Dad still read to us at night, when he wasn't too tired, and Mama was doing well.

My little brother, Grant, was getting around pretty fast, and it was my job to keep track of him. One day, he decided to pick-up his little sister, and he dropped her. Mama was upset. I got scolded, as did Grant, and I was told to watch him better. Our baby sister must have been made of good stuff, because the fall didn't ever seem to bother her at all.

Sis had made good friends, and for once our life had seemed to settle down. Of course, there was nothing on the radio except talk of war, but at the present time, it did not seem to affect us very much.

Chapter 11

Our Last Stay in the Mountains

It was time for school to be over for the year, and one night after supper, instead of reading to us, Dad sat down with us all to talk.

He said, "I have some news for you. I don't know if you will think it is good or bad. The bad news is that we will have to move. I know you've made friends, but this is necessary, and we will continue to see Uncle John and his family. We won't be going that far away. The good news is I have finally gotten a job on the railroad. This is work I know and like, and it will give us security again. Now there will be a couple of weeks before we have to move, so I thought since we all love the mountains so, I see no reason we can't camp a couple of weeks up in the Jemez. How does that sound?"

We were stunned. Sis and I were both happy with school here, and we had both made friends. We really weren't thinking of moving again. We looked at each other, and both had the same thought. We really didn't want to say anything because we knew Dad had looked for this job for a long time, and we could see how happy he was."

Mama said, "That sounds wonderful to me. I would like a couple of weeks in the mountains."

Sis and I both tried to look happy, although I thought the end of the world had come. I hated to move again, now that Little John and I got to see each other almost every day. I felt like I got hit in the stomach. I think Sis felt the same way.

Again Mama packed our best keepsakes away in the big trunk, including my book and drum. We did all we could do ahead of time before we had to move away. We sat aside the essentials we needed for camping and loaded them into the car. We locked up the house, and drove past the Jemez Indian Pueblo, past Sulfur Springs and the Soda Dam, and happiness just flooded us all.

Dad drove up to what we use to call Site Number Three. The old shacks that we stayed at years ago had finally fallen down, and the old barn, where I ran the nail through my foot, was not in much better shape than the shacks. Dad looked around and found some floors in pretty good shape. Apparently they were used by the CCC camp, and just left there. We sat our tent up on one of them, and that would be home for a couple of weeks.

Mama settled the two little ones down, while Dad, Sis, and I went to the spring for water. I was glad Dad went with us. Being out without him did not appeal to me, since this was very close to where I had seen the mountain lion when I was younger. As the three of us walked along to the spring, it felt good. The mountain air was clean and fresh. For the first time, since we had left the mountains, we all really felt at home here.

Mama had started the camp stove, and cooked supper. After eating, we cleaned up, and watched the sky as darkness enveloped us. The stars looked close enough to touch them. The night was so dark and quiet. It wasn't long before you could hear the noises of the mountain quiet being shattered by the hoot of the owls and the sounds of night. Dad threw a good size log on the camp fire, and we pulled up the covers of our bedrolls, and peacefully slept.

Our two weeks in the mountains flew by. It seemed like we had barely arrived before it was time to pack up again and return to Bernalillo.

When we got back, we were devastated. Mr. Pena had been watching for us. As soon as he saw us drive up, he came to the house and explained to Dad.

"Bill, I'm sorry, but while you were gone someone broke into the house, and everything is gone. We had gone to Albuquerque, and when we got back, the front door was broken down, and the house was empty. I'm sorry that happened."

"Ricardo, I know that it was not your fault. You have always been good to us, and have always taken good care of everything we left here. Don't worry about it. I know it would have never happened if you had been here. You have always been very kind to us. We would never blame you for this. We just want to thank you for all you have done. You've been a good friend, and please do not let this upset you."

Mr. Pena shook Dad's hand, and returned home. We went into the house. Mama stood in the middle of the living room. She covered her eyes, and just cried.

She said, "Bill, I can understand someone taking things from the house. I know people are in great need, but why would anyone take our pictures? They would have no use for them. Sure I can see, blankets and rugs, anything useful, but why pictures? Some of those pictures can never be replaced. We had pictures of my grandmother, when she was a little girl, standing with my mother when they lived in England. We had pictures of our children when they were just babies. We had pictures of the cars at the only family reunion that we ever had when everyone came to Colorado. Then there are the Christmas bulbs that my grandmother had given us. How many times have we had those on our tree, year after year? These are things that you just cannot put a money value on. Oh, this just makes me sick."

Dad said nothing. He put his arms around Mama and just stood and held her. After a while Mama, pulled herself together, turned to Dad and said, "I guess you better pull those bedrolls out of the car. We will sleep on the floor here tonight. We are leaving tomorrow anyway so don't pull out more than we need."

It was a sad night at our house. As we lay on the floor in our bedrolls, thoughts ran through our minds. We were all trying to remember the things that we had packed away in that big, old trunk for safety: Mama and Dad thought of pictures. Sis thought of the handmade, tatted handkerchiefs that Grandmother had given her. I thought of my book and drum that I enjoyed so much. Of course, then there was the old trunk itself, the one that Mama and Dad had been given when they were married, and the little table cloth that covered it when Sis and I used it for a table for special occasions. There were other things that could never be replaced.

When we woke up in the morning, Uncle John was at our house and invited us over for breakfast. He had heard what had happened, and besides they all wanted to see us off.

We knew when we left that we would not see our old friends as much as we were use to, but we also knew we would see them once in while.

A New Tomorrow

When we were all packed and into the car, we were a gloomy bunch, except that Mama seemed to be far away. She seemed to be deep in thought. There was not much talk among the rest of us as Dad drove on and on. We had left the green river valley and the land turned to low, rolling hills, covered with juniper and cactus. It was somewhat of a pretty area. It was different than the desert area, and even more different than our beloved mountains. Finally we began to see low, rolling mountains. Dad said, "We are getting to the Ortiz Mountains. That is where we are going. They are different than the high mountains. It will not be green and there will be few trees. It will be dry and quite rocky. It is coal mining country. Both anthracite and bituminous coal are found there."

"What is that, Dad?" I asked.

Anthracite is a hard coal. It burns hot and is much cleaner to burn than bituminous, which burns easily, but it leaves more pitch as a residue. Bituminous coal burns with a smoky flame – not as clean burning as anthracite. Bituminous coal is also called soft coal. An interesting thing to me is that anthracite is so hard, shiny, and pretty that it is sometimes used as filler in rock gardens and that sort of thing. It reminds me a little bit of the rock around La Bajada Hill."

"Are we going to stay here, Dad?" Sis asked.

"This new job is a very good job. It looks like it is a long term thing. The pay is better than any I've had since the logging camp closed. It seems to offer a lot as far as family life, and I think we will stay here for a long, long time."

"Tell us more about it, Dad."

Dad answered, "First let me tell you something about the area. The road we are on actually runs through the entire town. In fact if you just stayed on it, you would end up in Santa Fe."

I asked, "Is that the same Santa Fe where Father Lamy built his church – from my book, Dad?"

"Yes, Sis, that is the same one. Our house will be right on this road. That section is paved, and is a tree-lined street with wooden sidewalks. It's a pretty street. There is a big, cottonwood tree right in our front yard. The house is white, with green trim, and there are rose bushes in the side yard, and a drive way on the other side. There is a four foot high stone wall behind the house, and a hill behind that with our garage at the top of that hill."

Dad continued, "The house itself has two bedrooms, and a big porch. There is a living room, a dining room, two bedrooms, a big kitchen, a glassed in back-porch, and an indoor bathroom with a cast-iron tub. There are electric lights, and a coal furnace. There is a wall-telephone, but that will be used only for my work. There are only three telephones in town – one at the main office, one at the mine owner's house, and the one at our house. The reason we have one is that telephones are solely for town emergencies. I have to take the train to Waldo for water whenever it is needed. That is why the telephone is used only for business. Well anyway, I think you will like your new house. It is the best one we have ever lived in. Another thing, the school is close, and you both can walk to school. One of them is a new school, built by the WPA."

It was getting late in the day. Dad found a nice place to get off the road, and he pulled over for a break, and to take time for something to eat.

As we had been driving, Mama had been quiet. She had been thinking. She ate a few bites of her sandwich and said, "I think this is a good time to talk about something important."

Dad nodded toward Mama, and she continued. "Since yesterday, we have been acting like a bunch of whipped pups – feeling sorry for ourselves because we lost most all of what we owned. I know it was a blow to us, because some of it had sentimental value, but we are forgetting some very important things."

Mama looked at Dad and said, "When we got married, we thought we had a wonderful future. We expected a good income, a house, children, and security. Then the bottom fell out of every thing, and this country was hit by the greatest disaster ever – the Great Depression. When the logging company shut down, life seemed pretty hopeless, and dismal. It was almost impossible living on no income, and at other times our meager income was a real challenge. This is not to complain. We always had enough to survive, and I'm grateful for that."

Looking at us she said, "We would never have survived without the WPA, and the odds-an-ends work your father always found. As you know, many people were far worse off than we were."

Dad stopped eating, and Mama had our full attention as she continued, "I feel we need to look at the theft in a completely different light. Think about this:

When the White Man came to this part of our country, the Indians assumed the White Man thought the same as they did. The White man assumed the Indians had the same values they had. Indians had roamed the land at will and had always used what they needed, but never took more than they needed, nor ever wasted anything. The Indians assumed the White Man would do the same; however, the White Man came riding horses, and carrying fire-sticks, and killing many buffalo only for their skins. The Indians were horrified. The Indians depended on the buffalo, and they could not phantom the waste and the killing, and finally they started to fight back. They did not want their way of life destroyed, so they fought with a vengeance."

"On the other hand, the White Man thought the Indians were stealing when they took sheep or anything else the White man owned. The Indians thought that was fine, as long as they needed it, and made good use of it. The White man thought different."

"For many years Indian wars were fought simply because neither side took the time, or the interest, to see what the needs and the expectations of the other people were. There was much bloodshed over simple misunderstandings of different values. If only people would be a little more patient and caring, just think how much more would be accomplished in this world. Maybe we should put ourselves in that other person's shoes before we jump to conclusions. Just think of our own situation. I wish that whoever broke into our house had thought about what some of the things they took meant to us before they took everything."

Mama looked almost embarrassed but there was a light in her eyes as she continued. "Maybe we need to look at things differently. When you think about us losing our things, just think, they are only things - it is just stuff. Maybe whoever stole them needed them more than we did. Actually, I probably would have given them something, if they had just asked. Anyway, what was stolen is gone now. We will probably never recover any of it, so we need to simply put that behind us, and move ahead with our lives."

Dad slipped his arm around Mama, smiled at her, and said, "I think you've covered all the fundamentals, and you are absolutely right. When it boils down to it, whatever happens to us in this life, cannot always work out as planned. The depression is not completely over, war is looking us in the face, and here we are just starting from scratch. We face new challenges, new times, and what we do and how we grow will come down to what we do for ourselves and our attitude. We are going to a new job, a new town, new schools, new friends, and essentially a new life. I think we will do well. It seems to me that all we have gone through is simply living."

Mama said, "Last night I had a dream and I would like to tell you about it."

Dad answered, "I'd like to hear your dream. We have time. We are almost there. Go ahead and tell us."

147

Mama nodded her head and said:

"I dreamed I was sitting on a huge rock, high in the lush, green mountains. Every fiber of my body knew that there was reason to hope.

Then in the distance I saw a strong, healthy, vibrant man, walking alone, and standing straight and proud. Somehow I knew he was the spirit of Anasazi, one of the ancient ones, an American red man. These were the people who had walked this land thousands of years before we were here. He seemed serene and at peace with the world. Then he was joined and walked with three other men. They were men of all colors.

As I watched them, I thought, What a blessing it is to have more than just one flower in your garden, many kinds and colors, with each complimenting the other, and bringing untold joy and charm into the lives of all those who experience the work, the living, and the miracles of human life.

Then my dream went back to the four spirit men. They were of different ages, different cultures, with different histories and customs, yet they were all men of virtue, incorruptible, and with uprightness. They were people of integrity and with good principles. They were all of what made Anasazi. These were the spirits of our ancestors, yours and mine, who had lived and worked to preserve the beauty of this world, worked to keep the air clean and pure, worked to preserve the green mountains, and kept the water untainted. These were spirits of men who had respected man and the earth as something sacred. These men understood that you do not have to think alike, or to be alike, to be an important page in the long book of mankind."

Mama smiled at us and said, "Well, that was my dream. My thinking is if I had my choice, heaven would never be a city of shimmering gold streets. In the next world, I would want my spirit to walk the same sacred land of natural beauty that had provided for mankind from the beginning of time - before man had become burdened with greed. After time eternal, my greatest hope would be to find this world as green, lovely, and healthy as it was when man first began to walk upon it. I would like it to be as God made it - the ultimate plentitude of peace and substance."

Dad said, "Well, that was some dream! I think that you just gave us a lot to think about. I like your dream. To me it says: A man is a man, nothing more, nothing less. Time is flying. We better get back to today. Life doesn't wait for us, so let's move along.

Come on, Kids, hop into the car. We have a new life ahead of us, and we have a lot to do."

Finis